INCUBATING
Creativity
AT YOUR LIBRARY

D1615816

INCUBATING
Creativity
AT YOUR LIBRARY

A Sourcebook for Connecting with Communities

**ERINN BATYKEFER
AND LAURA DAMON-MOORE**

ALA
Editions

CHICAGO 2019

ERINN BATYKEFER earned her MFA degree in writing and her MLIS at the University of Wisconsin–Madison. She is the author of *Allegheny, Monongahela* (2007) and coauthor of *The Artist's Library: A Field Guide* (2014) with Laura Damon-Moore. She cofounded and edited the Library as Incubator Project from 2010 to 2017, and was named a *Library Journal* Mover & Shaker in 2014 for her work. She lives in Pittsburgh, Pennsylvania.

LAURA DAMON-MOORE has an MLIS degree from the University of Wisconsin–Madison. She is currently a community engagement librarian at the Central Library of the Madison Public Library. She has spoken on community engagement and creativity in libraries for the American Library Association, the South by Southwest conference, and several state and county library associations. She was named a *Library Journal* Mover & Shaker in 2014 for her work as cofounder and editor of the Library as Incubator Project. In 2014 she coauthored *The Artist's Library: A Field Guide from the Library as Incubator Project* with Erinn Batykefer.

© 2019 by Erinn Batykefer and Laura Damon-Moore

Extensive effort has gone into ensuring the reliability of the information in this book; however, the publisher makes no warranty, express or implied, with respect to the material contained herein.

ISBNs: 978-0-8389-1862-3 (paper)
978-0-8389-1878-4 (PDF)
978-0-8389-1902-6 (ePub)
978-0-8389-1903-3 (Kindle)

Library of Congress Cataloging-in-Publication Data

Names: Batykefer, Erinn, author. | Damon-Moore, Laura C., author.
Title: Incubating creativity at your library : a sourcebook for connecting
   with communities / Erinn Batykefer and Laura Damon-Moore.
Description: Chicago : ALA Editions, 2019. | Includes bibliographical
   references and index.
Identifiers: LCCN 2019007158| ISBN 9780838918623 (paper : alk. paper) | ISBN
   9780838918784 (pdf) | ISBN 9780838919026 (epub) | ISBN 9780838919033
   (kindle)
Subjects: LCSH: Libraries—Cultural programs—United States. |
   Libraries—Activity programs—United States. | Libraries and
   community—United States. | Arts—Library resources—United States. |
   Libraries—Marketing—United States.
Classification: LCC Z716.4 .B34 2019 | DDC 021.2—dc23
LC record available at https://lccn.loc.gov/2019007158

Book design by Kimberly Thornton in the Garden, Freight Text Pro, and Freight Sans Pro typefaces. Cover image © chamillew / Adobe Stock.

♾ This paper meets the requirements of ANSI/NISO Z39.48–1992 (Permanence of Paper).

Printed in the United States of America

23 22 21 20 19   5 4 3 2 1

EB: For David, for reminding me that writing
is the most important work.

....

LDM: For my dad, a wonderful communicator
and connector across departments and disciplines.

....

Both: We dedicate this book to all of the artists and
librarians who contributed to the Library as Incubator
Project for seven years. Your stories shaped our vision
of what libraries and librarianship can be.

contents

preface

WHEN YOU THINK ABOUT CREATIVITY IN LIBRARIES, WHAT comes to mind? Fine art books, coloring pages, Minecraft? ArtBots, a sewing class, a local music festival? Any variety of things probably comes to mind, and what *does* come to mind also varies widely between your colleagues, not to mention what occurs to the folks in your community. Every library, every community thinks differently about creativity and the role the library can play in a creative process. By and large, libraries *want* to be creative hubs. You want to offer access points that invite your community to learn new skills and expand their networks. You want to inspire, to engage. So how do you create a coherent, recognizable platform of access points so that your patrons can get the information they need, at the moment in their creative process when they really need it? How do you build, say, a platform that offers a local writer access to a historic newspaper database to find primary sources about the Spanish Influenza Epidemic of 1918; helps to spruce up her manuscript via the critique group that meets every Tuesday in the community room; and, using the current edition of *Writer's Market*, identifies publishing companies and literary agents; and finally, organizes a public author signing when the book is published.

This hypothetical writer is not going to waltz into the library and accomplish all of these items in one visit; each of these access points will be used over many months and even years. Some of your patrons may know that all of these steps can be accomplished at the library, but what about the non-power user, or even the nonlibrary user? Is there a way to shake up *your* thinking about the way you approach and market your library's resources and services in order to make it really easy for anyone to determine how they can use the library in their creative work?

We know there's a way. It's not perfect, but we dig it because it's scaleable, and is inherently customizable to your library. Most importantly, this approach helps you go beyond just *responding* to community needs into actively building a platform *with* your community. This is not a book about what equipment to buy, or what books to stock, or how to design your space. Instead we're going to work with what you already have going, what's already working, amplify it, and talk about some options for filling any gaps that you identify along the way. You can pick and choose what to use and how you use it.

This book came to be for a few reasons. In 2014 we wrote our first coauthored project, *The Artist's Library: A Field Guide from the Library as Incubator Project*. That title was really geared toward library *users,* with some ideas and hands-on materials for library workers. This time around, we're pleased to offer up some great ideas, ones that came out of our seven years spent collecting stories about the arts and libraries, to the folks who actually work at the desk, coordinate events and programs, and make decisions about what equipment to buy. We wrapped up active work on the Library as Incubator Project in November 2017, and this new book feels like an appropriate way to close out that project.

We're not claiming to be revolutionaries when it comes to library thinking and practice. We did not invent creativity, hands-on programming, or finding aids. In our Library as Incubator Project, what we were able to do was to connect with and talk with a *lot* of creative people, many of whom work in libraries, and collect those stories in a central place. When you start looking at all these individual stories, eventually you start to see themes and areas of potential growth that you just might miss otherwise. Unlike when we started the Library as Incubator Project, we also now have several years of professional library work under our belts—and definitely a much better sense of the practical, day-to-day workings of public and academic institutions.

While this book is certainly geared toward library workers who spend their days at the public service desk, in a program room, or putting the finishing touches on brochures and websites, we *especially* have in mind the worker who has encountered a "we can't do that" or "this is the way we've always done it" attitude from anyone at her institution, be it a supervisor, a colleague, or a board member. We sincerely hope that pulling together existing elements and filling in the gaps with community-driven additions is an easier way to build a creativity platform at your library than buying a bunch of expensive, underused equipment or throwing thousands of dollars at underattended and time-consuming programs.

We had a lot of fun writing this book, and we hope you have fun using it. Please stay in touch and let us know what questions you have, your successes, and your challenges—and what we've missed or could use work on ourselves. Thanks for taking this all in.

acknowledgments

WE'D LIKE TO THANK ALL THE CONTRIBUTORS TO THE Library as Incubator Project website, our coworkers and friends in the library world, our incredibly supportive families, and our mentors from the University of Wisconsin–Madison iSchool, who let us invent not one but two independent studies to develop our ideas and our website when the Incubator was just getting started.

We'd also like to acknowledge the following people, without whom this book would not have come together—these folks contributed everything from chunks of text and big ideas to weird art, moral support, gab sessions, and conference hijinks as this book came together.

Mallory Arents, Darien Public Library

Rachal Duggan, Madison, Wisconsin

Erica Grossman, Anythink Libraries

Dan Hensley, Carnegie Library of Pittsburgh

Janie Hermann, Princeton Public Library

Kelly Hiser, Pittsburgh, Pennsylvania

Ann Miller, Mead Public Library, Sheboygan, Wisconsin

Trent Miller and Carlee Latimer, Bubbler @ Madison Public Library

Sara Radovic, Jacksonville Public Library

Angela Richardson, Madison, Wisconsin

Catherine Royalty, Los Angeles Public Library

Holly Storck-Post, Madison, Wisconsin

Finally, a huge shout-out to Patrick Hogan at ALA Editions for his interest and support.

THE CREATIVE LIBRARY PLATFORM

WHEN WE STARTED THE LIBRARY AS INCUBATOR PROJECT as library school students at the University of Wisconsin–Madison in 2010, we wanted to answer one question: how do libraries serve artists? The question came up in one of our introductory classes with a wonderful professor and librarian named Louise Robbins, who opened a discussion on how different libraries work to serve everyone in their communities. We discussed tools and services for older adults, for children, for job seekers, for parents, for people of color, for people with disabilities, and for new immigrants and English-language learners. The list went on, and every time we considered a new subset of our vibrant communities, someone in class had an example of best practices in action or an idea from their experience or from the course readings.

That is, until we asked about artists.

Did anyone know anything about how libraries serve artists? Was there an article or an approach we had missed? Wasn't it interesting that "artists" were a group that could overlap with every other library user group we had talked about? Both of us are artists—Laura is an actor, and Erinn is a writer, and both of us mess around with lots of different creative practices, from cartooning to oil painting to crochet—so we were interested in how our hoped-for profession lined up with our artistic work. But no one knew of any standard approaches to supporting artists in a library context.

Louise knew exactly what to do: she proposed that we find out for ourselves and report back. And when we had scoured the literature and found not much, she suggested doing an informal survey and creating our *own* literature.

<1>

So we did.

We got in touch with a variety of local arts organizations in and around Madison and asked them to share our initial survey with their members, and we reached out to many local artists we knew or had some connection with to solicit their answers. At first, we figured we'd collect a hundred surveys from artists, examine the intersection of their work and their library use, and publish the results. But then the answers started rolling in, and they were *fascinating*. Artists used their libraries in so many different ways, and their answers to our final question, *What would your ideal library look like?* were glimpses into what the library as an institution *could* be. There was also a pattern to the answers that suggested a greater (and frequently unmet) need than any one particular artist's wish for a library with lots of natural light, flexible space, 24/7 access for whenever the muse struck, and stacks arranged for serendipity and happenstance. There was *something* there.

We knew we had to share these ideas and answers, and solicit more of them, in order to figure out what that *something* was, so we figured out how to build a website, and we created a Twitter account for the project, and we started sharing what we found. What followed was a tidal wave of interest that turned the Library as Incubator Project from an independent study into a serious volunteer side hustle. We had amazing conversations on social media, and published new interviews and stories from artists and librarians all over the country and the world every week—sometimes every day. Apparently, there were lots of people who had wondered the same things we had, who had stumbled over the possibility that there was *something* more to serving artists in the library space.

One of the things we learned from all of these case studies and conversations was this: we weren't necessarily talking about artists as a narrow set of people who show their paintings in the Venice Biennale (though we did talk to several of these). We aren't art critics; we're library workers. We needed to consider scope in a way that would be functional in a professional setting. Just who were we trying to figure out how to serve? Was there a way to make the library a supportive environment for all kinds of creative work, to support the full gamut of artists ranging from the casual hobbyist to the seasoned professional?

This was an ongoing conversation that evolved as we learned more from artists and librarians and from studying creativity and learning models. One of our heroes is Sir Ken Robinson, who wrote *The Element* (2009), which explores the nature and origin of creativity by examining case studies of highly successful creative people—from dancers and musicians to writers and even inventors and businesspeople. Robinson was a speaker at the Wisconsin Science Festival around the same time we were working out what the library-as-incubator concept *meant.* In his lecture at the festival and in his famous TED talks online (which we devoured), Robinson shares these basic facets of creativity:

- Creativity needs to be encouraged.
- Creativity is not "for" a "special sort of people." It is inherent in everyone.
- Creativity is a process that can be taught and learned.
- Cultivating a space for creativity is about "climate control." Given the right circumstances, opportunity, and attitude, creativity has a shot.

These ideas shaped how we thought about our project; we realized that the *something* that our interviews suggested was missing for artists in the library space and Robinson's "climate control" were one and the same thing.

In response, we expanded our definition of "artist" to include anyone who uses a creative process and physical or digital tools to make something new—whether that "something new" is a literal artwork or something more abstract, like a business model or process. This move opened our conversation to match the idea we started with: that "artists" as a user group could include every other user group that libraries serve. Makers and tinkerers, nerds and geeks, teens and seniors, professionals and dilettantes of every stripe—all of them could be artists in the library space, and their creativity could be supported and nurtured no matter what their information need or lifelong learning goal is. When we talked about the "Library as Incubator," we were talking about the library as an environment where you can create the right circumstances—through space, materials, and synergy—for creativity to take hold and develop. In short, creativity is expansive, inclusive, egalitarian, and nonjudgmental, and it belongs to everyone. It belongs in our communities. It belongs in the library. And if we as librarians could support creativity, we could improve *every service we provide.*

Creativity isn't necessarily about *making* anything. It's about *thinking* differently.

Your library team, whether they consider themselves artists or makers or not, can train themselves to think more creatively because creativity is inherent in every person, and using it is a skill that can be learned and developed. Again, no one is asking you to paint the Sistine Chapel ceiling or compose arias—we're asking you to try some exercises, think a little differently, apply what you learn in your library work, and see what happens.

You might be surprised—and delighted—by the results. Because that's what creativity does: it surprises. It delights. And isn't that what all of us need more of? In our jobs, and in our lives, we could all use a jolt of unexpected, thought-provoking delight that makes lightbulbs turn on, elegant solutions become clear, and exciting collaborations and possibilities emerge.

A few notes before we begin:

For simplicity, when we use the term *librarian* in this book, we are talking about a library worker who may be an MLS-holding librarian, a library assistant, or any of the many varieties of professional or paraprofessional job titles that crop up in the library world. We've been, and we've worked with, all sorts of library workers who are doing great things in their communities, MLS or no. So we're going for the cheapest grammatical solution—*librarian*—the one that doesn't require convoluted sentences with a laundry list of options every time we want to make a note of a library-job-holding human who is doing her job.

Again, for simplicity, we often use a composite *we* in our anecdotes about our personal experiences of the Creative Library in action, even if only one of us was there. We do this simply to avoid the ridiculousness of saying *I, Laura Damon-Moore,* or *I, Erinn Batykefer,* when giving an example—we want you to be able to read this book without parsing sentences to figure out what we're saying.

As we mentioned, we also came up with our own definitions for some of the words we use regularly in this book. *Artist* is one of them. We define it broadly to include anyone using their inherent creativity in a deliberate (though sometimes unconscious) way to come up with something new. *Creativity* is another word we define inclusively, as an inherent trait that manifests in thinking differently when solving problems, whether those problems are figuring out a new work procedure, or considering balance and color while editing a photograph.

Let's also talk about the term *platform*. In utilizing that term, instead of *initiative* or *program*, we're inspired by several pieces of work and thinking in the library world that use this term; specifically, David Weinberger,[1] R. D. Lankes,[2] and writings from the Aspen Institute.[3] Our vision for the Creative Library platform, which we explore in this book, is that it functions as a vibrant collection of resources, people, and experiences that the community can utilize and participate in during their creative process. Whether the need is space to work, research materials, help navigating a newspaper database, or a place to showcase the artwork or writing or performance when it's done, the library is a free and accessible place to do all of that.

We envision this book as being most useful to folks who work in public libraries where programming is a component of their work, either actively, by planning and running programs as a living part of the collection, or more passively, by being aware of programming as a service and being able to make connections between program offerings and patrons in order to meet their information needs. We believe that any librarian will be able to get something useful from reading this book, but we acknowledge that youth services folks have a different focus and scope—and quite a lot of programming approaches already baked into their jobs. This book is intended to help everyone else reorient their work in a similar fashion, for the betterment of all library services, from high-flying festivals and in-depth programs to the humble and necessary book drop check-in.

Ultimately, we believe that *every* department in every library could benefit from a larger, profession-wide philosophical shift toward the Creative Library platform, and we want to help you find ways to make this happen in your library. That's what this book is about: pulling together the core ideas from hundreds and *hundreds* of interviews, program models, and approaches to service delivery that we shared on the Library as Incubator Project website for the last seven years, and distilling them into concepts and models you can use, remix, and remake into something that works for you, your staff, and your library.

Our goal with *Incubating Creativity at Your Library: A Sourcebook for Connecting with Communities* is to identify the elements of the Creative Library platform and guide you through the process of pulling out and packaging those elements in order to offer a whole-library approach to creative exploration and experimentation. This is not about starting from scratch. Rather, it's about surveying your community, your collections, your team, your activity calendar, and even your building, to see what's already going on and what you have to work with. We want to ask you: how do these existing elements interface with what's already happening outside the library, in your community? Are there duplicate programs that can be trimmed or "reverse-piloted" in order to free up staff and space? How can you expand your work with community groups and individual patrons and determine what new or additional elements are wanted to flesh out what you already have going?

What makes the library a creative hub? Is it an abundance of rotating artworks in an airy gallery space? Is it having an oversized book section packed with expensive art reference materials that are available to anyone who can come in and use them? Is space the key—having a variety of spaces that visitors can use, from studio tables that invite messy activities to quiet study spaces with whiteboards and dry-erase markers for brainstorming and collaboration?

In *Incubating Creativity at Your Library: A Sourcebook for Connecting with Communities,* we're thinking about the library as a multifaceted, engaging platform of opportunities that people (both visitors and staff) can make use of as they see fit. Some people may visit to explore the reference books about fish one week, and workshop their newest short story with a writer's group the next week. Visitors may take advantage of the library from many different angles: attending workshops, checking out materials, or just finding a quiet space to work.

It can be easy to get wrapped up in the specifics: what equipment should we buy for the makerspace, and what programs will attract the most attendees over and over? Instead, this book will help you approach the work of building the Creative Library platform starting with what you already have: on the shelves, on the calendar, on your staff.

What are the main elements we're going to explore?

ELEMENTS

Resources

Resources are otherwise known as the "stuff" that people have access to through the library. They are the books, periodicals, DVDs, audiobooks, music, and more that are on the shelf. They're also the stuff that is not necessarily on the shelf but is still available with a library card or via a curated resource list; e-books, digital audiobooks and music; and access to research databases, digital collections, and online newspaper archives are standard resources.

Space is another important resource for the community. In library buildings, space means anything from quiet work or study areas, to small rooms and tables built to encourage collaboration and group work, to larger community rooms where events such as workshops, performances, and author readings can take place. Think about spaces within the library that are underused at the moment; but also consider whether there are outside spaces that are available to you. Even the sidewalk can hold opportunities. The process for reserving and using these spaces depends on your library, of course—but when you make it clear that this important resource is available and bookable by the community to promote their creative work or collaborate with others, you can include space as one element of your Creative Library platform.

Equipment is also an important resource, and one that varies dramatically from library to library. It includes the basics (public computer stations and Internet access) as well as the professional-grade media lab or makerspace. Much has been written and documented about library makerspaces, along with best practices, equipment lists, and so on, so we're not going to focus too much on that conversation in this book. Our general advice is to make sure to work with your community before purchasing a lot of new equipment. If you can, pilot some ideas on a small scale first to make sure that whatever you're committing to is going to be worth it. Are your sewing workshops filled to capacity every month? It might be time to invest in a permanent machine or two. Or maybe it's a couple of digital recorders and some tabletop microphones that people keep coming in to use or check out. Maybe you should invest in some higher-quality recording equipment—or purchase some in partnership with another library—and organize some hands-on workshops on recording and editing in order to "level up" the learner experience.

Activities, Programs, or "Invitations"

When it comes to "getting creative" in the library, the conversation frequently focuses on the hands-on side of things. Call them what you will—programs, events, workshops, activities, participatory opportunities—these are the *invitations* to expand the creative side of your brain. An invitation could be a hands-on, get-messy workshop where you learn something new or dive more deeply into a particular skill. Examples include everything from stop-motion animation to podcasting, and from pottery to knitting. An invitation could also be a lecture series that features artists in the community talking about their research process, with a reference librarian on tap to discuss a relevant resource or some aspect of the nonfiction collection. It could also be an independent activity table that provides a break for busy students or gives your regular weekday visitors a chance to exercise a different part of their brain.

These invitations are the backbone of the Creative Library platform, and we guarantee that there's already stuff on your calendar that fits the bill. Our goal is to show you how to extend these invitations more deliberately, and match them to other traditional services in order to effectively leverage both of them. Of course, we'll also share some great examples of engaging invitations that we loved from the Library as Incubator Project, and offer some recommendations for how to approach planning new ones.

Partnerships and Engagement

On the Library as Incubator Project website, PARTNERSHIPS and COMMUNITY stand out as two of the biggest tags in our tag cloud. There's a reason for this. The Creative Library platform is most engaging, most exhilarating, and most creative when community partnerships, ideas, and feedback are integrated directly into the platform. Some libraries have an official or formal approach to engagement with the community, while others rely more on one-on-one relationships or historical partnerships. But whether you're working with formal agreements or contracts or using a more casual approach, it's important to document the work and cultivate partnerships so that when opportunities arise, you're in a position to move forward easily and efficiently (though this does not necessarily mean *quickly*, as we'll discuss later).

On this subject, we're dedicating chapter 6 in this book, "The Lenses: Community-Led Invitations," to community-driven and community-led Creative Library ideas in order to demonstrate the opportunities for growth that can be gained when you fling open the doors of the library to a project or program that is not organized down to the minute by librarians (we say this with love; *we are* librarians, and we love order, clocks, spreadsheets, and, yes, control). Let's take a step back and consider a couple of ways that libraries can cede some of their power when it comes to program planning and the development of resources and services. Inviting your community to utilize the Creative Library platform and make their own visions happen, rather than using a prescriptive "we know best" approach, is highly beneficial for library staff as well. You'll have a chance to see your workplace being used in new and exciting ways, and you'll be able to pull from past experiences to create even better events and services in the future.

Library Staff

No matter how robust or well-curated a library collection, it's necessary to have library staff who can help make connections between library users and the information (on the shelf or otherwise) held by the library. Library users who are working on creative projects *need* expert assistance to connect with information that can enrich their creative work. This places reference work and research help comfortably in the Creative Library platform. Do you have an opportunity to share the recommendation-for-purchase process or interlibrary loan resources with the creative people in your community? This brings collection development staff and resource-sharing departments into the Creative Library platform. When library programmers curate and package workshops and activities (or "invitations," as we're calling them here) that support creative practice and skill development, they're contributing to the Creative Library platform. Outreach or engagement staff who develop close partnerships with arts organizations or individual art-makers and who collaborate to mutually grow capacity and support the work are also an integral part of the Creative Library platform.

A quick anecdote: Laura works as part of an amazing team of public services staff at the Madison Public Library's Central Library. The MPL is home to The Bubbler, an arts and creativity platform with a vibrant screen-printing component. One of Laura's colleagues, L., is a dynamic reference librarian and part of the library's collection management team. One day L. spotted a longtime patron working at one of the study carrels on a project she recognized from previous interactions: drawing images of vintage cars onto a T-shirt. Even though L. does not work directly on Team Bubbler, she made the link between this patron and a library resource that he had access to but was not aware of previously. L. connected the patron with The Bubbler program assistant, who could then give him information about the equipment he had access to—including the screen-printing equipment and training that were available in The Bubbler room. This patron, Lonnie Evans, would go on to not only create more work in the Bubbler room, but would also get to know Bubbler staff and even have an exhibition of t-shirts and prints installed at Central Library in the spring of 2019.

L. spotted a way to "level up" this patron's work by connecting him to a free resource located in the same building, in much the same way that, in a typical reference interview, one might suggest a relevant database in addition to the print material a patron initially requests. This is library business as usual, helping to connect people with information; this is just considering the library in a holistic, whole-library way, with staff being familiar with resources across departments and being comfortable making those resources known as part of a reference or research transaction.

We'll also put in a pretty serious plug for library managers and administrators to offer invitations for the folks who work *in* the library, as well as library visitors. In the same way that interdisciplinary academic work can lead to a cross-pollination of ideas and a deep exploration of new (and old) intersections, we're championing the idea that time and permission to make something new, to work on your own creative projects, is an important part of library work and staff development. How can we support our coworkers and our staff in their creative endeavors?

LENSES

Community-Led Invitations

An important approach in this model for library platform development is the idea that whenever you think about incorporating a new service, resource, or invitation into the Creative Library, you take a moment and ask yourself whether this addition is community-driven or community-led. Think of the "community-led" question as a lens that you look through every time you're considering whether to launch a fancy new invitation or initiative. Has anyone actually asked for this new piece of equipment that you're considering? Are you seeing a gap that the library could fill because of conversations you've had with patrons and non-patrons in and outside of the library? Do you have committed community partners or individuals who are excited to work with you in order to bring this new invitation or initiative to fruition?

Evaluation

Similar to the concept of "community-led" invitations, we want evaluation to be a question that is on your mind all the time, as another lens through which you examine each element. Is there an evaluation plan in place? Are you measuring outcomes to see if you're reaching your larger institutional or strategic goals? And, more broadly, what are the goals that you have for the larger Creative Library platform? How will you know if and how effectively those goals are being met?

THE CREATIVE LIBRARY PLATFORM IN PRACTICE

One thing that happened during the course of the Library as Incubator Project was that we heard a *ton* of stories about successful creative platforms from libraries and communities of various shapes and sizes. In chapter 8, "The Creative Library Platform in Practice," we've pulled a whole slate of them together. This chapter is a selection of the examples that really fit what we're talking about and which demonstrate that the Creative Library platform will look and operate differently depending on your library, your staff, and your community. That's why we dig this model so much—it's not prescriptive; instead, it can be customized to your library and your community. The assets you have to work with are already there. The examples we share here are not exhaustive, but they're hopefully a starting point, a good baseline for you to start to frame your own platform.

PACKAGING IT ALL TOGETHER

You've taken a step back to survey the existing resources and have identified the ones you want to promote as part of the Creative Library platform. You have examined the activities or invitations already in place that fall into the Creative Library category, and worked with other staff, partners, and community members to identify some new activities to pilot. The staff across departments are aware of the creativity-focused resources and services happening in other parts of the library or at other branches, and they feel confident in speaking about these with patrons. But, how are you to take the elements of the Creative Library and package or brand them in a way that makes sense to patrons and also does not require a ton of extra staff time and work? In this book we'll take a close look at a couple of different approaches, and also touch on a handful of documents and practices that will make your life easier once the Creative Library platform gets up and running.

We've touched on the elements of the Creative Library platform and the various lenses you can apply to each. Now it's time to examine the four platform elements (Resources, Invitations, Partnerships and Engagement, and Staff) and the two lenses (Community-Led Invitations and Evaluation) in depth, in the chapters that follow.

Notes

1. David Weinberger, "Library as Platform," *Library Journal*, 137, no. 18 (2012): 34–36.

2. R. D. Lankes, "Library as Platform," https://davidlankes.org/new-librarianship/ new-librarianship-master-class-mooc/ilead-usa-and-new-librarianship-course -content/week-3-libraries/library-as-platform.

3. Aspen Institute, "People, Place, and Platform," 2014, http://csreports.aspen institute.org/Dialogue-on-Public-Libraries/2014/report/details/0087/Libraries.

THE ELEMENTS: RESOURCES

ANY LIBRARIAN WILL TELL YOU THAT THE LIBRARY HAS never been about *books*—not really. It's about *information*—the ways people find it, the ways they use it to learn and explore, to inform and shape their lives, to create new things. The skeleton of the library is its collection of resources, and that skeleton hangs together based on how we as professionals work to provide the most complete and diverse representation of quality information that we can. Books may be our brand—the spine of most collections—but the truth is that we find many ways to connect the people in our communities with information: books and magazines, games and films, tools and toys, and hands-on experiences and gatherings where folks can meet up, connect, and learn from one another. We'll talk about books, yes, but we'll also talk about digital resources, library space, equipment and technology, and even *people* as part of the resources that can be shared and utilized in the Creative Library platform.

Public libraries are institutions that promote lifelong learning, and as librarians we do that job best when we acknowledge that people learn differently. Some are happy learning just by reading, and a robust and well-tended collection will satisfy them. But many of the skills that people wish to learn require more, and this is where our collection development skills may be applied in new but no less rigorous ways to build invitation calendars that offer entry points and opportunities for learning experiences, just as our physical collections do.

We also consider different user groups when we build our collections or rearrange the library space. How will we accommodate *everyone* in the community? The children? The older adults? The business people? The teens? The differently abled folks?

<13>

Creative practice in libraries offers a chance to consider new learning methods and opportunities to connect patrons to one another through a shared interest, and thereby connect them with information we couldn't provide access to in any other way. The mutual exchange that takes place in a workshop or skill share between teacher and student is a very particular kind of learning—one that is largely endangered in our assessment-obsessed school system and is virtually nonexistent outside of formal—and often expensive—training or instruction. By considering artists and how your services can better respond to their needs, you can improve service to *everyone*.

The library is a place where the resources needed to explore an idea, remain informed, or learn a new skill are accessible and free—that's not a new concept. Providing entry points for creative learning is not fundamentally different from the practice of building other traditional library collections. The skills you already practice to create lively and evolving collections of gardening books, documentaries, or popular magazines are relevant here. What the Creative Library requires are some new and different rationales for *why* a particular resource is something the library provides. To be sure, libraries host some wonderfully offbeat collections (cake pans? other human beings?[1] fishing rods?), but reconsidering the uses of collections that are already in place—reframing their worth to your community in terms of how they support creativity—can reveal hidden possibilities and make the library as a whole more flexible, responsive, and accessible because it's responding not to a specific need, but to a global need that everyone has: to incubate their creativity.

In this chapter, we'll share a variety of examples of resources that libraries can consider "creativity fodder." Most of these are in your collections already, and just need a fresh perspective to see them as engines of the creative platform you're building. We include some examples from real-life libraries that make their regular collections something special and surface their items to those patrons who are seeking creative inspiration in innovative and interesting ways.

THE ARTIST'S IDEAL

One of our favorite questions to ask the artists we interviewed for the Library as Incubator Project website was, "What does your ideal library look like?" The folks we asked were self-identified creatives—artists and makers of all stripes—so peeking into how they thought about the library and its resources seemed to be the best way to figure out what libraries were already doing well and to imagine what we could do in the future. We got a huge variety of thoughtful answers, from the whimsical and weird to the practical, and every wonderful idea in between.

We've included a few examples of these "ideal library" answers in each section below as a kind of benchmark, not only as a crowd-sourced snapshot of how working artists, makers, and other creatives think of these resources in the library, but also how they want to use them, what they wish were possible, and what they wonder and dream about when someone asks "what does your ideal library look like?" Not all of these answers make sense when you have to balance them against such common challenges as tight budgets, limited staff, and practical concerns like insurance and liability or the needs of other patrons, but that's the wonder of creative thinking: when you remove the roadblocks of what *is* and think about what *might be,* you often stumble on something new and interesting in between that really could work.

We encourage you to think *what if* here, and throughout this book—and not just for the pleasure of fantasy. We'd like you to think practically: *what would it take to make this work at my library?* Who would be interested in it? How could you make something like this happen? The stakes are low here—you're just *thinking.* We know there are many librarians out there who are dealing with situations where resources of all kinds, from humans to dollars, are scarce, and it's easy to feel that all but the most basic, known-quantity services are out of reach. We'd like to offer this alternative perspective by way of encouragement: sometimes the most elegant design comes about *because* the materials are limited. If you only have two colors of paint to work with, you're more likely to experiment with different applications, textures, or mixtures than if you had an unlimited palette at your disposal.

You can do this. You already have plenty to work with.

PRINT COLLECTIONS

[My ideal library] would be large and open and inviting, with warm and quiet and comfortable areas for study and work 24 hours a day, 7 days a week. On a purely selfish level, it would be within walking distance of my home and studio, but I would also want it to have general appeal and accessibility because this is how we all benefit from the serendipity and exchange of information and ideas—through contact with people and books and programs. Stacks would be open, and would include a variety of standard reference books as well as information specific to all manner of technical, scientific, literary, historical, cultural, spiritual, philosophical, and aesthetic concerns and subject matter . . . There would also be an area devoted to artists' books, and we would be permitted to read and handle them. Information about the artists would be available nearby. Also books related to book arts, and information about book-related resources and facilities. Programs could include a series of salons with artists talking about their work. Plus, of course, this particular collection would provide a market point for book artists.

—*Carol Chase Bjerke, photographer and book artist*

The collection . . . [in my ideal library includes] a comprehensive art and design history [section], with plenty of cultural studies, sociology, architecture, economics, psychology, urban studies, theatre and performance, and history thrown in too. Diverse and unusual publications—artists books, zines and self-published works. An approach to purchasing that is really active and engaged so the contemporary is well represented as well. And journals, newspapers, magazines. . . .

—*Clare Qualmann*

Books

The public library may be the best possible place for an artist to nose around in stacks of books to find inspiration. Wandering through the stacks, enjoying what photographer Carol Chase Bjerke calls the "tactile pleasure of running hands over spines," and the serendipity of finding unexpected or overlooked titles and taking them home are all things that artists noted as creativity-sparking aspects of the library's resources; these are ways to support intuitive leaps, mind-wandering, and interesting connections that creatives might not make otherwise. Some artists even suggested that their ideal library would be a little difficult to navigate, with OPACS tucked away (so you'd be more likely to just browse first), endless archives you could get lost in, and stacks arranged by associative groupings rather than the Dewey Decimal System (though you could argue that Dewey can sometimes feel like free association already).

Obviously, these kinds of changes aren't practical in a space that must serve both the frazzled parent's quest for a quick meals cookbook and the artist's desire for desultory exploration and happenstance. But there are ways to do both: the neat stacks can furnish oddball book displays with broad criteria like "Hasn't been checked out in two years" or "Black and white and read all over," where fitting items must feature a black-and-white cover design, no matter what the subject. Creating an interesting visual hodgepodge in a book display can satisfy some people's desire for dissonance, happenstance, and serendipity in their browsing experiences, as well as provide the added bonuses of boosting circulation stats and giving excellent but infrequently checked-out titles a Hail Mary.

The library's breadth of book offerings can also be a catalyst for new ideas—sometimes artists beg for breadth that borders on the archival, with first editions moldering on the shelves for eternity. Without Hermione Granger's undetectable extension charm, most public libraries without a specific research focus to their mission have to weed regularly. But this doesn't mean you can't accommodate breadth. If you're part of a library system where patrons can borrow from other libraries, or if you have a good interlibrary loan procedure in place, consider promoting those services in the stacks where your offerings are necessarily limited to the greatest hits, or where patrons are often asking for more. If you have a subscription to a digital resource that digs deep—archival newspapers, genealogy resources, or in-depth science or literature databases—these can be great ways to extend your collection with a bit of judicious marketing and a knowledgeable staff.

Consider ease when promoting these kinds of resources—is it possible for your staff to learn five-minute demos that they can do on command when someone asks at the desk? Is there a demo you can automate as a screen saver for in-stacks OPACS? Does your library have a YouTube channel? Can an intern make a video or series highlighting interesting resources with a mini-demo you can pull up at any time, or share on social media? Try to make an artist's browsing experience—in the library and remotely—one of discovery and exploration, even if your collection is smaller than her imagination (and remember—there is *no* collection big enough for the average imagination!).

Magazines, How-to Books, and Practical Guides

In their responses to the survey, artists often fantasized about a library space with unlimited resources that would stock beautiful and unusual materials that are relevant to their practice or their curiosity. Ephemera like zines, artist books, obscure first editions, and niche literary or art magazines often cropped up on our respondents' wish lists. Sometimes these types of things are hard to collect. Subscriptions to literary magazines, for instance, often cost a lot more than the slam-dunk subscription to *Real Simple* that circulates till it disintegrates, and these magazines often publish only twice a year. That's hard to accommodate in a serials budget that is slowly being swallowed by rising subscription costs for the *New York Times* and its coveted and much-copied crossword puzzle.

Public libraries *can* respond to these wishes, though—if not with full archives of *Art in America* readily available on the shelves, then with some creative accommodations that focus on something we do quite well: *community.* Our communities are often the key to making decisions about what to buy: "if it circulates, it stays" makes sense to a degree, but what about "live here, shelf here"? Local interests can help you build Creative Library collections *and* connect patrons with what's happening in their hometowns. In Pittsburgh, for example, there is a vibrant community of writers, from poetry and fiction to screenwriting and comedy. Building a local authors section into the 811s, for example, makes sense in a place with not one but two well-known MFA programs in writing and a regular rotation of poetry readings, festivals, and events in the area. Local literary magazines like *Pittsburgh Review, Creative Nonfiction,* and *Hot Metal Bridge* might be worthwhile print subscriptions, even if your regular readership is small, and especially if your library hosts a writers' group. Seeing local work on the shelves can help your patrons feel they belong in the library as artists, too.

Zine fests, ComiCons, partner exhibitions of book arts, and digital or lending access to weird and wonderful first editions and obscure texts can make a small, strapped public library vast. You might not have the budget to accommodate every chapbook or zine made by a local maker, but consider how you can make the library a welcoming place for those voices. Hosting local authors for a workshop, panel, or book-signing event can be a meaningful way to connect and welcome them. Ask for donated copies—they'll probably be signed!

We also recommend getting input when it comes to finding creative solutions to the problem of collections and access—passive or active input, or a combination of both. As we saw time and again in artist interviews, folks are often delighted to share their ideas and recommendations, especially when there is an imaginative wish-list quality to the ask. What books and magazines would artists and makers want to see on your shelves? They'll tell you if you ask.

Libraries often collaborate with education groups—schools, community colleges, tutoring services, and so on—to get book lists that they should have because patrons in their area will need them. So why not ask arts centers, community college art departments, and local art and music teachers for their suggestions on book lists? If you have a great crafting section, consider finding your local quilt guild or bonefolders guild and asking them about the books they value for their craft. You may be pleasantly surprised that your trusty Desk Reference pointed you in the right direction, but you'll often find that local interests can be particular, and you inadvertently have a collection with a blind spot. Baltimore Album Quilts are famously difficult to make and quite lovely, so you may have resources on them in the textile history section, but not necessarily in the how-to crafts books. If you're in Baltimore, though, you might need to—there's a specific guild for contemporary quilters who make that style of quilt in your area: the Baltimore Applique Society. They may tell you their favorites if you ask. As a bonus, folks in craft guilds or art societies love to talk about their passions—and they will likely tell their guild (or invite you to share at one of their meetings) about what you have at your library and how you can help them specifically with their craft. It's a win-win situation.

SPECIAL COLLECTIONS

We consider programs, or "invitations," a resource unto themselves—*lots* more on that in coming chapters—but sometimes they are a great way to make sure your community knows about your special collections that don't often see the light of day. Jessica Pigza's experience as a rare books librarian at the New York Public Library is a lesson on how to effectively surface your library's best stuff— even if that stuff is in the Restricted Section—by piggybacking with other well-used services.

Jessica, in partnership with other staff and with a slate of renowned designers and makers in New York City, organized a series of activities that was part exhibition, part workshop called Handmade Crafternoons. Instructors would facilitate hands-on activities while Jessica and her colleagues would pull relevant items from the library's special collection to showcase the library's unique resources while also teaching a new skill.[2]

ARCHIVAL MATERIALS

Many libraries also function as the de facto historical society or local archive for their community. This is one of those "under the radar" collections that might not immediately spring to mind to include in a platform dedicated to creativity. But local history rooms and collections, no matter how small, can be a real treasure trove for people doing research about a particular time period or who are looking for inspiration in photographs, newspaper clippings, and ephemera like menus or broadsides.

Melissa Mannon, the mastermind behind the *ArchivesInfo* blog, wrote up some ideas for how to use archival materials, in particular "orphan" (i.e., unidentified) photographs, as inspiration for new creative projects:[3]

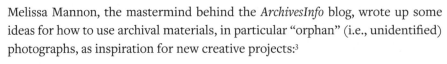

Though these materials have limited value in libraries and archives for research purposes, such materials can provide visitors with unlimited fodder for the mind. While orphan images may not serve a strong research role, they certainly have a secondary role to play that may be more valuable in encouraging the general public to gain interest in what archives and library special collections can offer.

As a librarian or archivist, do you have unidentified photographs in your collections? Consider placing them prominently. As a library media specialist, I plan to make copies of the images in my personal orphan photo collection. I will stick them in a box for students to paw through, talk about, write about, and make collages. As an archives consultant, I encourage my clients to do the same in their archives. You can place copies of images on counters to generate some interest in primary source materials as objects of discussion and inspiration.

Are you an artist looking for inspiration? Ask your local librarian if she has orphan photos or unidentified images in her collection. Use the images to loosen writer's block or to build whole novels. Consider using the images in collages, prints, and other visual arts too. Copyright laws give you the right in the United States to use these "abandoned" images.

—*Melissa Mannon*

PRINT RESOURCE TAKEAWAYS

- **Local authors.** Local writers and artists with publications should be represented in some way on your shelves! Collection development folks will tell you that self-published items are often of lower production quality than those traditionally published, with thinner pages, covers, and a shorter shelf life, and that can mean high turnover. But the proliferation of publishing options (both print and digital ones) and the critical lack of #diversebooks and #ownvoices in major publishing houses means that many authors— local or not—are finding ways to reach readers by publishing themselves, and it may be worth allocating some collection dollars for self-published materials of interest, even if you have to replace them a bit more often. Digital can also be a good option here, especially if you have a high-quality e-content platform.

- **Oversize books.** Consider allowing these to be checked out if you don't already. It's hard to enjoy a big, beautiful coffee-table book in the library. Circulate them. We completely understand that some limits on circulating *very* big books are in place for safety and practicality reasons: it's too hard to manage delivery between branches and system libraries when the books won't fit in the transport bins. If that applies to you, consider allowing in-house checkouts. Many ILS programs have sophisticated options for cataloging books so that they will not show up on the holds list, but are indeed available for checkout. Let folks take those big books home—the travelogues, the catalogues raisonné, and the nonstandard shapes and sizes are all interesting. Some libraries avoid buying them, but these are often books by and about artists. You want them on your shelves. Artists need to see themselves there.

- **Patterns, directions, how-to books.** If oversize books are a bit of a pain, books with huge fold-out patterns, detailed directions, maps, or extra content online can be wonderful resources for artists—and a headache for the processing department. Consider how your library can best make these accessible. A hand lettering book with lined pages for practice is a bit useless sitting on the shelf with a giant Day-Glo sticker that says DO NOT WRITE IN THIS BOOK. Can your library allow patrons to copy such pages free of charge? Can your Day-Glo sticker include instructions for how to use the copy machine for best effect? How can you help keep materials in good shape for everyone to share *and* still accommodate the practice necessary to explore and learn a new skill?

DIGITAL COLLECTIONS: THE UP ALL NIGHT ARCHIVE

My ideal library is open 24 hours a day and has books available right on the shelf (a lot of libraries in New York City have most of their collections in storage), so you can slumber party with your favorite book. My ideal library has a big fireplace in the middle where everyone meets to read books in cozy reclining armchairs till four in the morning. It's very quiet there, and the whole place smells like the inside of a Steinbeck first edition.

—*Josephine Decker*

Man, my ideal library has everything, is infinite and is perfectly preserved. I guess therefore it'd be unusable, but I really dislike getting rid of books and hate seeing libraries discard materials (except insofar as I am the recipient of these discards—I'm a collector of old dictionaries and old ephemera and books, something that shows up in the magazine I edit, *DIAGRAM*, which features a lot of old schematics and diagrams). Nothing would be weeded unless I willed it. And it wouldn't just be books. Video games in particular continue to be important texts for me, and I try to keep many of the ones I remember best, even if they're no longer playable. Still, the box art on, say, the game *Starflight* is enough to prompt emotions as vividly as remembering a read-through of a novel I loved when I was fifteen.

—*Ander Monson*

One of the most interesting patterns we saw over seven years of asking "What does your ideal library look like?" was that creative people wished the library was open an accessible 24/7. This is great news for libraries that have digital collections, because those collections make the library's open hours 24/7—just like all those creative patrons have wished for. It also opens up opportunities to create resource pages specifically for creative types—and anyone else who may be interested—of freely accessible digital resources from other research institutions and libraries. Many academic libraries at universities with a special claim to fame will share their institution's best stuff digitally, and there is a wide variety of nice collections big and small that are available online.

Here are a few of our favorites, plus some places to search for new ones:

- Digital Public Library of America: Use the browse by topic section (https://dp.la/browse-by-topic) to find lots of interesting collections in one place. The Online Exhibitions are also excellent.
- Smithsonian Resources
- NYPL Digital Collections
- Library of Congress
- Biodiversity Heritage Library

As podcasts continue to gain in popularity, you can curate a collection of podcast titles that are related to creativity and the arts. This is a great opportunity to apply a "community-led" lens to resource-sharing. You can crowd-source favorite podcasts from patrons and share them online as a "listen list" the same way you would a booklist.

You can promote additional electronic resources that your patrons have access to with their library card—databases of digitized newspapers, historic and literary reference materials, medical information, all of these and more may be just what a writer or artist needs in order to move their project along to the next phase.

SPACE: THE PHYSICAL LIBRARY

> My ideal library will have space for sounds to disappear into, room for all sizes of events, an outdoor courtyard, windows to look out of, windows to look into, large selections of a variety of titles, places to sit down comfortably to read, places to sit down comfortably and have conversations with other people, places where you can eat and drink, places where you can get food and drinks, places where objects and artwork can be displayed, places where multiple functions can be held without impacting the other functions, places where ephemera and rare books are collected and made available to the public.
>
> —*Daniel Wuenschel*

> Places of silence and light. Libraries are perfect for my art, because they are places of quiet and contemplation. Time slows down in a library. It's an ideal space for enjoying the slowly changing colors and patterns.
>
> —*Peter Erskine*

Space was another consistent wish for artists and makers imagining their ideal library. They asked for large tables, areas for quiet contemplation, and space for noisier collaborations. They saw the library as a workshop, a studio, and a gallery, with areas where they could create new work, areas where they could teach others what they knew, and areas where they could share and show what they'd made.

Almost every artist surveyed who commented on space asked for two things: quiet and natural light. Sometimes they also asked for noise, or spaces where they could collaborate without disturbing others, but light, light, light was primary. Consider your space right now—not the space you may be able to renovate in ten years. Is the most climate-controlled, creative seat in the house stuck in the stacks? Is the best natural light shining on a bank of personal computers, when they would be better in a glare-free zone?

Try out a different configuration for a month (and expect a little bit of insecurity from some folks who are anxious about change). Nudge your workspaces into more creative-conducive configurations: mash smaller tables together to make large ones, get them under that skylight, make that space a silent area—or make it fair game for quiet conversation. Put out a coloring book and colored pencils. Or utilize an outdoor space by setting up a worktable in the sunlight and inviting people to use it when they ask where they can work. Simple shifts like this can make a huge difference to how creative patrons—who need to see color saturation, assemble robots with fine tools, or just read and enjoy good light—feel welcome.

Interestingly, creature comforts cropped up in artist responses as well—there were many requests for fireplaces, comfy chairs, and cafes where one could get a cup of coffee or a snack. Oh, and permission to eat in the library as well. Think: Gryffindor common room. Your patrons are human beings, and if they're spending a great deal of time in the library, it should be a comfortable space that welcomes their bodies as well as their minds.

Larger meeting and community event spaces are also on the table. Space is an important resource for a lot of groups that may not have a physical location—theater companies, music collectives, artist guilds, and the like. Is your meeting room policy able to accommodate ad hoc groups or unofficial groups that are interest-based? For people who just need a place to meet, this may be something you can easily accommodate with a few tweaks to your space policy.

And of course, what if your library already has a dedicated makerspace or studio? That's absolutely part of your Creative Library platform. You might want that room or space to be the central component of the platform, or you might decide to include it as just one of the many resources that make up the platform. Use this "platforming" work as an opportunity to look closely at that space and do some assessment on what's working and what the challenges are at the moment.

Many libraries already have gallery walls or posts where art may be hung. These may be formal or informal, separate or integrated into the high-traffic areas. This kind of space is a natural fit for the Creative Library platform. Make sure people know how to submit their work for consideration, and make sure that staff know where to direct people when they ask.

EQUIPMENT

Equipment is another area where you may have some money to spend and the artist community can help inform your decisions. Laser cutters, 3D printers, and other resources are *expensive*, which means that if you have the means to supply access to them, many artists will be delighted to use them to prototype their designs without shouldering that cost. But if you don't have this equipment—and most libraries don't—consider what *is* affordable to you, and whether there are options for access through other means, including partnerships. The Madison Public Library, for instance, held off on purchasing 3D printers when the first wave of 3D-printing mania hit the library scene, and this was because they had developed a great partnership with a local makerspace called Sector67. This makerspace already had several 3D printers and a 3D scanner, and the folks there were willing to bring that equipment to library branches for demos and make-and-take programs; the library chipped in for materials, and a knowledgeable Sector67 volunteer was on hand to troubleshoot the famously persnickety printers. As a result, patrons could still explore 3D printing, many learned about Sector67 for the first time, and the library didn't have to invest right away in technology that was expensive and potentially flash-in-the-pan before they knew their patrons really wanted it long-term.

The Arrowhead Library System (ALS), a small system of seven libraries in south-central Wisconsin, came up with an ingenious solution to the need for makerspaces in its libraries. Each library couldn't afford to renovate and equip spaces to meet the needs and interest of its community, so they joined forces, applied for an LSTA technology block to fund equipment, and created a shared Mobile Makerspace for the system's seven libraries. System team member Melody Clair was the point person for the Mobile Makerspace and was in charge of ordering equipment, managing the Makerspace website and documentation, and coordinating scheduling and deliveries. To determine what equipment should be included from the get-go, Melody sent systemwide e-mails to libraries in the ALS asking for input on what kind of maker equipment the staff felt would be most useful and interesting for their patrons, and she put together the kit from there, with the intent to add and replace equipment as the program got up and running and staff could gauge more specific recommendations and interest from their communities.

The library staff submit requests for equipment online, and system staff review all the requests and fill in the calendar personally to ensure that there is enough time for delivery to and from the system's office and to make sure the equipment is ready to go to the next library. The equipment "lives" at the system office, and is delivered by book bin to the seven libraries in the ALS. All documentation is online and available via the Mobile Makerspace website, so staff can check there for troubleshooting help and equipment manuals. This is a great example of the small-but-mighty public library finding creative and cost-effective ways to meet people's interests by sharing resources across libraries that can't purchase their own.[4]

Partnerships with other organizations may also be of use here. Artists often have particular asks, and often artist groups or organizations struggle to meet their members' needs for certain kinds of space and equipment. Local artist groups might be a great resource, not only to suggest some of their favorite magazines if you're reevaluating your subscriptions, but also to do some bartering. What if your library and the local woodworkers guild could purchase a piece of equipment jointly? Or write a collaborative grant? Your local organizations may need things you can barter for with them, like space, or a venue to show their work or teach skills. Prioritizing their members' use of new equipment in exchange for expert program workshops and volunteers to help patrons learn to use the new equipment could be an invaluable way to make a special resource viable.

PEOPLE: COMMUNITY MEMBERS AND LIBRARY STAFF

> My ideal library has a million places to plug in your laptop, and if you ask the librarian in charge to let you film your dance video in the religion section, she always says yes.
>
> —*Josephine Decker*

> My ideal library has an incredulous amount of diversity. There are people of all races, religions, and ages, and there are programs to honor these differences. There are opportunities for authors and artists like me, who are just hoping to be a part of the conversation and offer some fresh perspectives. There are books that reflect my story, my lineage and ancestry. There is powerful art on the walls that stops you dead in your tracks and makes you question yourself and your thought process. There is community engagement, artist talks, and a coffee shop would be the cherry on top. But that's wishful thinking, I know.
>
> —*VersAnnette Blackman-Bosia*

> My ideal library offers a space for people to come from the community to not only read about other's adventures, but learn about themselves, to dare to grow and dream, make new friends and laugh. An attached bakery with the scent of coffee might be nice too!
>
> —*Danielle Bonney*

People are the engine that make the Creative Library work. When we conducted presentations and workshops at the Library as Incubator Project, we often emphasized the "library as incubator" idea as fundamental to library service.

Stripped down to just one sentence, every library's mission is to connect *people* with *information*. But the thing about *information* is that it's slippery. Beginner cataloging courses in library schools often have at least one interesting class session when the discussion of making information "findable" drills down to the (surprisingly controversial) question of what information *is*.

Is a research paper on cheetahs information? Sure. Everyone can agree: you can learn from an article; that's a decent criterion.

Is a cheetah itself information? . . . Yes? No! Maybe?

The truth is that information comes in many packages (even without wild beasts), and people seek, find, and use information in different ways. People—our patrons and our staff—learn in different ways as well, and might seek out a different information package depending on their needs.

Let's take the 738s:

You can learn a lot about the practice of making pottery by reading a book or watching videos. Perhaps you love the closed forms by Toshiko Tokaezu, and you watch a documentary on her work where you get to see her practice, burning paper in the bottom of her pot to dry the clay enough to add each huge slab, layer by layer, till she's standing on a stool above the wheel, shaping the top of a massive form. Perhaps you flip through a retrospective of exhibitions and installations of her work and notice a progression in her choices of color over her career, or how her sculptures' shapes respond to the environment when they're made for outdoor installations.

All of this learning is valid.

But a physical artistic practice like the ceramic arts demands a different kind of information exchange in order to learn how to *throw* clay the way Tokaezu did to make her huge drum-like forms. You will have to get your hands very, very dirty to learn about centering and pulling clay into shapes. It's a kind of information that is learned by your body as well as your brain, and the mode of exchange isn't a book—it's *another person*. An art instructor demonstrates how to wedge a lump of clay to make sure there are no bubbles, and how to center it on the wheel. You watch and then try it yourself, and the instructor gives helpful tips and encouragement as you match what you see with what you feel, physically, in the act of working through the steps. You screw up. You try again. You get it right, and the instructor tells you to remember what that *feels* like, so you can replicate it next time.

This is workshop learning, and there are many kinds of information that are best delivered in this form, ranging from experiments, messy activities, and critiques to second and third chances. So, as librarians, how do we make this kind of information findable? How do we connect our communities with the information *inside people's heads?* The potter's expertise isn't fully accessible through books and films. What if your community really wants to understand it? You have to find a way to connect them with a person and with an experience that can flesh out the full spectrum of information in 738—Ceramic arts.

This is all to say that the information held by your community members and by your staff is possibly the *most precious* information your library has. It's nuanced and specific, and it's constantly evolving and growing. If you can harness the expertise and interests of *people*, your Creative Library can float along splendidly, even without tons of other resources.

We'll dive into this concept in more depth as we explore partnerships for community-driven programming and the practice of staff retreats and staff ownership in the program calendar, both of which leverage the knowledge and passion of your staff and your community to create exciting programs that draw people in because the instructor cares about what she is sharing.

In particular, taking care of your staff and building the goodwill connections that make the library a welcoming place for their creative interests pays dividends—both in job satisfaction, and in their knowledge of and engagement with the resources they need to understand in order to connect patrons. Take the extraordinary staff artist residency at the State Library of Victoria in Australia. One of their staff, a reference librarian named Dominique Dunstan, got in touch with the Incubator Project after having one of these *paid* staff artist retreats, where she transformed the staff area whiteboards into beautiful, ephemeral natural history illustrations, a series she dubbed the "Whiteboard Project."[5] Here's an excerpt from our interview with her:

Library as Incubator Project (LAIP): The Whiteboard Project came together because of a unique artistic fellowship hosted at your library. Can you tell us about that program? How did it start, and why do you feel it's important to support artists specifically in a library setting?

Dominique Dunstan (DD) : For the last decade, the State Library of Victoria has sponsored two streams of fellowships. There is an external program and a staff program. The external creative fellowships are offered annually to artists and scholars, working in any medium or discipline, who propose thoughtful and innovative ways to use the state library's collections. Since 2004, staff fellowships have been offered to members of the staff who can demonstrate that their project will have lasting and/or significant benefit to the library and to the staff member concerned.

The fellowships aim to:

- Promote the State Library of Victoria as a center for scholarly activity and research.
- Encourage scholarly, literary, and creative use of the library's collections and the production of publications or work based on them.
- Publicize the library's collections.

The principal benefit of the staff fellowship program is to give members of the staff the means and the uninterrupted time to work closely with the rich resources of the State Library of Victoria. Staff fellowships vary in length from one to three months, depending on the nature of the project. Fellows are provided with an office and are free of all other work duties for the duration of the project.

That the library encourages scholarly and literary use of the collection in this way is wonderful, and one might expect that. But the fact that the library welcomes and supports artists takes things to another level.

I think this program is visionary. It promotes and celebrates creativity, imagination, and innovation across disciplines and expands our perception of libraries as not just repositories, but as engines of cultural production and activity. The ways that we record and express our history and culture are evolving so quickly. The collaboration of artists and libraries seems a perfect relationship for capturing this process and gives meaning to it in a way that can be shared far and wide.

LAIP: You're a reference librarian, so you're trained to find information for all sorts of purposes. Did you find that your work as a fellow changed how you looked for project resources when your focus was creating art?

DD: It took me a while to reconcile my librarian and artist mindsets. This was a bit of a surprise, but the fellowship was full of surprises. Artistic inspiration is an omnivorous beast. Ideas and images come from the most unlikely places and you learn so much by doing, or "tasting," to continue the analogy. The information environment of a librarian is very orderly by comparison. It is full of protocols and systems. I had to find a way to let order and serendipity, the visual and the verbal, interact. Sometimes I would spend a long time pursuing a resource or line of research without much result, but when I moved to another approach the penny would drop, and something that I'd overlooked would jump out and take me forward. I literally felt like an explorer. Tangents, happy accidents, and the luxury of time let me see my resources with new clarity, and think about how and why I do things.

LAIP: Tell us about how the Whiteboard Project developed over the course of your fellowship.

DD: In 2012 the board of the State Library of Victoria awarded me the Jane Nicholas staff fellowship. This fellowship is offered in honor of one of our colleagues who passed away in 2010. It allowed me to spend three months on a research project of my own design and gave me a unique opportunity to combine my two major interests—art and libraries. The topic of my fellowship was "A Natural History of the State Library of Victoria": this is a personal discovery and visual document of a Victorian icon. I have worked at the state library since 1997, so it has been a big part of my life. There have been so many changes during that time, and there are no signs of things slowing down. It is very much a living library, and you don't need to spend much time here to realize that its evolution has been continuous and unstoppable. For these reasons, the theme of natural history offered a multilayered way of looking at the library and its collections, past and present, and to also look at the process of discovery and information-sharing in the days of the great naturalist explorers, as compared to today. Reading about this golden age of natural history, I was struck by the spirit of collegiality that united enthusiasts, collectors, scientists, artists, and adventurers around the globe. I wanted that spirit to inform my research and tried to think of ways to include the staff at the library and share my results.

The Whiteboard Project was one attempt to do this. For the first time in all my years at the library, I was able to spend hours and hours poring over treasures in our Rare Books and Manuscripts collections. The artwork, writing, and materiality of these early collections, journals, and sketchbooks were a revelation. It was an experience that I wanted to share in a way that would be immediate, personal, and open. I sent out a library-wide offer to create artworks on empty whiteboards in library staff areas. The artworks were to be based on early illustrations of native animals. The response was overwhelming, with many more invitations than I could fulfill. Originally I'd planned to do lots of quick sketches, but as I started working I became more aware of how people inhabit these spaces. I wanted to make work that respected this and contributed something of value. I also fell in love with the illustrations I was studying and wanted my homage to reflect their beauty and comprehension. This meant producing drawings that were more detailed and refined and of course took much longer, so there were fewer of them (ten so far). To offset the number of people I had to disappoint, I gave priority to communal spaces—kitchens, thoroughfares, open-plan areas—so that more people could see them.

The whiteboards were perfect for this project. They offered freedom to experiment in a way that might have been very difficult in public spaces. I could work on an ambitious scale without impacting the building or facilities; the staff could be part of the creative process as well as the outcome; and conceptually it gave me a medium to interrogate the nature of the office environment itself. In a play on the subject matter, I used materials native to the environment. Therefore I had to use dry erase markers, and a defining characteristic of the whiteboard is its transience. Conventional office materials made challenging art materials, however. The work was physically demanding, and technically difficult.

ADDING NEW RESOURCES

If you've looked at all your *stuff* and considered the creative platforming you can do to pivot what you have into what you want, and if funds are available in the form of reallocated budget, grants, or partnership dollars, then adding new resources may be in your future. Congratulations!

We certainly believe that you can build a Creative Library without *any* new stuff, but we never say no to a new line item, so we'd like to share some best practices for soliciting feedback and ideas from your patrons before you swipe that credit card. Here are a few ideas for crowd-sourcing suggestions from the folks you want to use the stuff you buy:

- Post a question on an interactive message wall for people to share their ideas on colorful Post-It notes. It's a fun, eye-catching installation for a few weeks and often garners some illuminating responses (and some weird drawings and possible profanity—make sure you can monitor it a bit).
- Make it easy for patrons to recommend new books and resources that aren't in the catalog. An online form should do the trick and should be easy to find on the library's website or embedded right in the catalog, so that an OOPS! We Don't Own That! message isn't a disappointing full stop.
- Check with other local libraries to see if they're interested in pooling money to purchase bigger items to share.
- Keep track of what people are already using regularly in the library in order to have a sense of what other items might complement what's already popular.

- Consider posing the question—just the one!—as part of a program or workshop evaluation survey to see what people want.

Again, get in touch with partner organizations, or organizations with whom you'd like to partner. If you are writing a grant, you're often required to have advisors for your grant proposal, and the same kinds of folks can help here: people with community clout, special expertise, or who are part of sister organizations can all be great resources. Then be a good neighbor and help them out when they are working on their own proposal!

Notes

1. Human Library, http://humanlibrary.org.

2. Jessica Pigza, "Handmade Crafternoons at the NYPL," 2012, Library as Incubator Project, www.libraryasincubatorproject.org/?p=2699.

3. Melissa Mannon, "Orphan Photos to Inspire the Arts," 2013, Library as Incubator Project, www.libraryasincubatorproject.org/?p=12099.

4. Laura Damon-Moore, "Mobile Makerspace at Arrowhead Library System," 2014, Library as Incubator Project, www.libraryasincubatorproject.org/?p=14326.

5. Erinn Batykefer, "Featuring: Dominique Dunstan & the Whiteboard Project at the State Library of Victoria," 2015, Library as Incubator Project, www.libraryasincubatorproject.org/?p=10971.

THE ELEMENTS: INVITATIONS

PROGRAMS . . . WORKSHOPS . . . HANDS-ON, PARTICIPATORY activities. Whatever you call them, what we're talking about here are opportunities for library users to engage with the library beyond a walk-in, walk-out transaction. For our purposes, we'll refer to these as "invitations," because that expands what we think of as library "programs" to include independent activities (which are sometimes called "passive" programs), as well as off-site activities and gatherings. In this chapter we'll take a look at several examples of invitations, and dive into the process of planning new ones.

GROUP INVITATIONS

This type of activity is what comes to mind first when we talk about library programming. The library organizes a workshop, markets it, community members attend it, and they come away with a new skill, and hopefully a feeling of being more connected with other attendees and their creative community. Sometimes the library is playing host to a group that is already connected, and sometimes the library is playing a more active role in orchestrating those connections. For our purposes, we will focus on the library-as-coordinator role in planning group invitations. There will be some crossover and more details in chapter 4 when we talk more about partnerships and the importance of community engagement in facilitating a richer, deeper library experience.

The following examples of group invitations are things we like to talk about because they're "easy wins"—it's not difficult, for example, to sell a library administrator on the idea of incorporating art-making into the tried-and-true library book club. But we chose each example as an invitation to participants to see their community, their library, and even a book club's book in a new and creative way.

Example 1: Pop de Fleurs at the Carnegie Library of Pittsburgh

There's a reason why the Pop de Fleurs project, which started in Pittsburgh in 2015, continues to be one of our favorites.[1] This invitation came out of a partnership between the Fibrearts Guild of Pittsburgh (the idea was conceived by guild member Annette Sandberg) and Suzy Waldo, the library services manager for the Carnegie Library of Pittsburgh–South Side. The Fibrearts Guild already had experience with a large-scale, citywide installation effort; a few years prior to Pop de Fleurs, the guild orchestrated an effort to "yarn-bomb" a number of Pittsburgh's bridges.

The collaboration between the Fibrearts Guild and the library resulted in a series of colorful public art installations around the city: sixteen library locations plus the main branch. In the Pop de Fleurs project, community members participated in systemwide workshops where they learned how to create flowers from recycled materials like fabric, ribbons, wool, plastic tablecloths, and plastic bags. The workshops went on the road, too, engaging people at schools, senior centers, homeless shelters—anyone who would host them. The flowers made in the workshops were then installed on the grounds and inside the libraries around the city in a variety of arrangements to showcase the work by community members. The best part? Pop de Fleurs is a *winter* installation that takes place in February, so it's not just an invitation to learn and make, but to come together and brighten neighborhoods. An unexpected and delightful pop of color blooms around each library, reminding residents that spring is on its way (and that the library is still there, with free DVDs to binge on winter weekends), just when Pittsburgh is at its most desolate.

Why we love this project:

- The threshold for engagement with the project is low. You don't need to be an expert in fiber arts to create a flower or two to contribute to the larger project.
- It involves a close partnership with a community arts organization. Rather than the library striking out on its own, Pop de Fleurs leverages the strength of the Pittsburgh arts community and the space of the library as a welcoming, collaborative environment in which to gather and make.

- The product was embedded in the community. The public art pieces that were installed as a result of the project were not only on display in the libraries, or in an art gallery or art center, but both in and outside of different community spaces, making the pieces accessible to passersby as well as library users.

How you can make a similar project happen:

- If you already have a relationship with a local arts organization or collective (which doesn't need to be fiber arts-related), reach out to them to see if they have any interest in working on a collaborative public art project. If they are, let them steer the ship as far as what the project is and how community members can get involved.
- Keep an eye out for announcements on social media and community calendars for public art or collaborative art activities happening nearby. Reach out to the organizers to offer the library as a workspace or as an outlet for promoting the activities.

Example 2: Poetry Invitations

Creative writing invitations are a natural fit for libraries, and there are lots of directions you can take. Poetry in its many varieties offers opportunities for library patrons to engage deeply with different aspects of the library's collection, and poetry's flexibility of style and form make it a welcoming way for patrons to start a new writing project.

Group workshops centered on poetry allow people to meet others with overlapping interests and can lead to collaboration and idea-sharing. Some of the workshop ideas are simpler to plan and facilitate than others. If the topics or depth of the workshop seem a little intimidating or outside of your comfort zone, try reaching out to the English department at a local university, college, or community college, or put out a call for local poets who are interested in facilitating some workshops.

- **Book spine poetry.** In this method of poetic composition, a participant grabs a bunch of books off the shelf, stacks them up, and the succession of book titles on the spines forms a ready-made poem. This technique is popular among youth services librarians and school librarians, and is also a low-pressure and entertaining entree into poetry for adults. Participants can do this activity solo or in pairs, and pretty much any area of the library works. You can even "write" poems during a tour of different collections: picture books, nonfiction, periodicals.

- **Redacted poetry.** A redacted poem is made by blacking out, or "redacting," most of the words on the page of an old or worn-out book. The remaining words and short phrases are then strung together to form a poem. Made popular by the poet Austin Kleon (check out his book *Newspaper Blackout* for a number of examples), redacted poetry is a way to repurpose discarded books or to engage in a new way with a book you already know. Make photocopies of the pages so that people can redact most of the page with black markers.

- **Ekphrastic poetry.** This is poetry that describes, interprets, or reflects on works of visual art such as paintings, sculptures, or photographs. This activity is based on a program kit created for the Incubator Project by the poetry collective Line Assembly.[2] It offers an opportunity to do a deep dive into the library's fine art books and oversized collection. (See Appendix A.)

Why we love these projects:

- All of the above examples make use of library items that are already available to you, no matter how large or small your collection. With few exceptions, every library has books, and every library has at least *some* resources in its fine art section. In a pinch, you can search online for digital collections of Decorative Arts, Fine Arts, or Art History and pull up or print out some examples for attendees to write about in their poems.

- Each of the examples offers an opportunity to pique people's interest in library books. By spending time literally in the stacks engaging directly with the material that's on the shelves, you're increasing the likelihood that someone will see something they want to take home and explore further. Before venturing out to the stacks, remind people that they are welcome to check out anything they find during their exploration.

How you can make these projects happen:

- As noted previously, poetry workshops can feel intimidating if you're not a poet or writer yourself. Feel free to ask for help from a more experienced instructor (but be prepared to pay her for her time—see chapter 4 for more on this topic), or embrace your own amateurishness by offering examples of your own work and being upfront about your lack of formal training. This can make the endeavor feel more accessible to everyone involved.

Example 3: Book to Art Club

Our next example actually got its start in 2013 as a sister project to the Library as Incubator Project. The Book to Art Club is a group activity that takes a very "library thing"—the book discussion—and incorporates a visual art-making activity as a key access point for exploring and discussing the work.[3] For this example, we hear from Ann Miller, the makerspace coordinator at the Imaginarium for the Mead Public Library in Sheboygan, Wisconsin. Ann was an early chapter leader for the Book to Art Club and is now the coordinator for the international Book to Art Club.

Around the same time that the Mead Public Library began actively seeking ways to meet its community's interest in the maker movement, the 2014 Wisconsin Association of Public Libraries (WAPL) conference was held in Sheboygan and featured "The Book to Art Club" presented by Laura Damon-Moore, Katie Behrens, and Holly Storck-Post of the Library as Incubator Project. The presentation was highly motivating, and the Book to Art Club seemed to be a natural fit for increasing both the Mead Library's maker and book club offerings in a fun and innovative way. The Book to Art Club's inaugural session (in 2014) featured Jasper Fforde's dystopian novel *Shades of Grey: The Road to High Saffron* and offered attendees the use of basic art supplies and a whole bunch of inspirational fodder related to Fforde's novel: a stereoscope as a leapback item, Ishihara tests, and Ishihara spoon cupcakes. That first session was held at the library in a meeting room with two cabinets of art supplies for pop-up makerspace activities.

Mead's Book to Art Club started its second year by partnering with the neighboring John Michael Kohler Arts Center's makerspace, the ARTery, for a special season opener that coordinated the club's reading of Erin Morgenstern's fantasy novel *The Night Circus* with a tour of the exhibit Carnival of Ink and an evening of printmaking activities. Mead's club partnered with the ARTery again that fall for a tour of Loy Bowlin's Holy Jewel Home: The Home of the Original Rhinestone Cowboy and a discussion of the NEA Big Read *True Grit* by Charles Portis, in addition to rhinestone and cowboy-themed art-making.

The collaborations with the Kohler Arts Center were so popular that Mead's Book to Art Club moved to the ARTery at the beginning of its third season and has been meeting there ever since. The third year was also the beginning of an annual summer collaboration with another neighbor, Bookworm Gardens. The first discussion was on the memoir *Lab Girl* by Hope Jahren, and the club pressed flowers into journals and examined collected specimens under microscopes. Yearly book discussions with tours and special projects designed by the ARTery or Bookworm Gardens continue and have become a way to keep things exciting for club regulars and to attract new members.

With the fifth season soon to begin, the Book to Art Club plans to celebrate with a year of members' personal favorites leading up to the five-year anniversary in October 2019, and hopes to continue collaborating with community partners to provide stellar Book to Art Club sessions for the community.

The Book to Art Club is ever growing, and with thirty-three clubs in existence nationwide. There are now clubs for juveniles, teens, and adults. Each Book to Art Club is as individual as its members. In addition to hands-on crafts, clubs have baked culinary art projects and brought props to enhance their discussions

Of note, the Camas Public Library in Camas, Washington, created camp merit badges and snacked on s'mores while deliberating over *The Interestings* by Meg Wolitzer. The Davis Academy in Atlanta, Georgia, made time-turner necklaces and sipped butter beer for the discussion of *Harry Potter and the Cursed Child* by J. K. Rowling, and the Columbia College Chicago Library focused on *Grimm's Fairy Tales*, rather than a single story, with each member working from fall until spring on their own handmade volume of Grimm's tales.

—*Ann Miller*

Why we love this program:

- For communities that value more "traditional" library services and programs, the Book to Art Club can be an effective gateway to introduce hands-on activities for adults through the familiar setting of a book discussion. It also requires minimal extra equipment and space: just a table or two big enough for art supplies, and chairs for participants.
- A Book to Art Club offers an excuse to reach out to local art educators in your community, in the same way that the Mead Public Library works with the ARTery and other community partners. In order to avoid over-asking or exhausting your art educator pool, pick a few books or activities that are easy enough to facilitate yourself, or have club members bring their own project and supplies every once in a while.
- The book discussion model is flexible, and you can do as little or as much as you like or have capacity for. If monthly meetings are too much, try a quarterly club, or have every third title in your library's regular book club incorporate a Book to Art project.

How to make this project happen:

- Tap into your book+art experts: youth services staff! Youth librarians have likely been doing art extension activities for years. Ask for their thoughts and whether there's even the potential for some intergenerational programming (older adults and youth, a family book club, or teen lit for adults).
- As noted above, use this as an excuse to reach out to your local art museum, art center, botanical garden, or a local artist collective to see what the partnership possibilities might be.
- Visit booktoartclub.squarespace.com for book and project ideas (there's no need to limit your choices to what's on the website, either) and register your chapter. Ann is available as a resource regarding logistics and how to get your chapter off the ground.
- Your Friends of the Library or the library foundation may be interested in contributing to an activity that supports both hands-on learning and traditional literacy activities. Ask for their help in purchasing supplies or providing honorariums for guest artists.

INDEPENDENT INVITATIONS

Independent or "passive" invitations require much less hands-on time from staff, and can be a good option for libraries that have limited programming space. You can make room for independent projects with just a tabletop, or even a blank wall and some signage to orient patrons. You'll want to check on the station on a regular basis to make sure that supplies and pieces are tidy and replenished as needed. If you have volunteers who are in the library on a regular schedule, include tidying up the area in their list of responsibilities.

Example 1: Draw the Library

A favorite recent artist in residence at The Bubbler at Madison Public Library is Rachal Duggan (also known as "RADIllustrates").[4] As the first official illustrator to be the featured artist in residence at The Bubbler,

Fig. 3.1 Draw the Library Checklist

Rachal got people all over the library making pictures and capturing moments through a variety of invitations. One of the invitations Rachal set up was a series of independent drawing stations that played into her workshop theme of Draw the Library. These stations, which were just small tables arrayed with paper, pencils, and pens, and a checklist of items for people to draw (see figure 3.1), ended up being a way for library patrons to contribute to a little zine that Rachal put together to document hand-drawn snapshots of the library space and staff.

Why we love this project:

- It is easy to set up and clean up, with little maintenance to do in the meantime besides making sure that the station is stocked with pencils and things are generally tidy.
- This invitation encourages patrons to look around and see the "everyday" library through a visual lens rather than just a transactional one.

How you can make this project happen:

- Make your own checklists for library patrons to work on and set aside some table space to use for walk-up stations.
- Plan to "publish" drawings that are left behind. This can be as simple as sharing images of them on social media or it can be more elaborate, like printing a limited number of "library zines."
- Combine the walk-up stations with organized group drawing/doodling/illustration workshops with a professional illustrator. Ask a local high school or college art department for a referral.

Example 2: Message Wall

Mallory Arents, the head of adult programming at the Darien Library in Darien, Connecticut, maintains a "message wall" made up of a blank wall, a stack of colorful Post-it Notes, and a prompt encouraging patrons to consider everything from "What kind of dog would you be?" to "Should we shelve the mysteries with the regular fiction?" Switch out the prompts every week or twice a month to keep the area lively. The message wall can be used as a way for patrons (and staff) to contribute to a larger conversation, and as a way to get useful feedback on a particular library operation.

Other variations on the message wall theme that we've seen include a Q&A or advice wall where patrons can post their own questions and conundrums, and can also offer up their own ideas and solutions for others. A subway wall covered in Post-It-sized messages in New York City became a kind of open group therapy session after the fall election season in 2016.[5]

When the Library as Incubator Project team was in residence at The Bubbler at Madison Public Library, we hosted a "word wall" where people could share their favorite words on old catalog cards and add them to the community word wall. The cards made for an invitation that was easy to transport to different areas of the building (use painter's tape for easy on-and-off), including a public elevator.

Why we love this project:

- For patrons who might not feel comfortable sharing their ideas with staff directly, the message wall or board offers another option for giving quick and easy feedback.
- Rather than a paper survey, the message wall offers a community space for people to see what others have suggested and add to or expand these with their own ideas.

How you can make this project happen:

- No wall space? Try a rolling whiteboard that can be pulled out and tucked away depending on your needs and other space constraints. With a rolling whiteboard, you can also try the feedback station in different areas, to see what yields the most Post-it Notes or comments.
- Make a plan ahead of time for how the message wall will be monitored and what to do if or when inappropriate content is posted on it.

Example 3: Community Puzzle Table

A classic independent activity, the jigsaw puzzle, provides an opportunity for patrons to exercise their visual and spatial functions.[6] The setup requirements for this invitation could not be easier; all you need is a tabletop and a jigsaw puzzle to get it started. Leave the finished puzzle out for a day before setting up the next activity, or break up the finished puzzle two or three times to give multiple rounds of puzzlers a chance.

Why we love this project:

- It couldn't be easier to plan for.
- It's ever-changing, but can become a familiar feature of the library with minimal effort.

How you can make this project happen:

- If table space is at a premium, put out the pieces on a roll-up puzzle mat for simple setup and cleanup.
- Ask volunteers to check on the puzzle table as part of their routine to make sure that puzzle pieces are picked up from the floor.
- Put out a call for puzzle donations on social media to make this project available at no cost to the library.
- Whether you source or buy your puzzles, consider your library's upcoming calendar in order to line up puzzles that relate to summer reading themes, seasons, local celebrations, holidays, or other events.

Example 4: I Draw New London

This example blends the independent invitation with the off-site invitation. The I Draw New London invitation at the Public Library of New London (Connecticut), which is headed up and documented by librarian Ellen Paul, invited community members to check out circulating drawing kits and draw images of places or things that were important to them as New Londoners.[7] The drawings and art supplies in the circulating kits were then returned to the library. The whole initiative culminated in a public exhibition of the drawings that celebrated New London from a variety of perspectives. The kits were checked out 50–60 times, though the number of finished drawings that came back was somewhat less. Finished drawings included places and community landmarks, household objects, people and pets, and things that defied categorization.

Why we love this project:

- The setup for the invitation is relatively low-pressure for staff: they purchase art supplies and notebooks, create instructions for the invitation, and work with cataloging staff to create basic catalog records needed for checkout of the drawing kits.
- People can do this invitation on their own terms and on their own timeline, rather than trying to hurry to finish something in a workshop.
- The outputs of the invitation, the drawings and the resultant exhibition, are both highly personal and community-building, both for the community members who did the drawings and for people who come to check out the exhibition.

How you can make this project happen:

- If your supply budget is strapped for cash, consider asking your Friends group or library foundation for support to purchase art supplies. Because this invitation has an open-and-shut timeline (say, six months from supply purchasing to exhibition opening), there's no need to worry about its long-term sustainability. A couple of hundred dollars should buy plenty of materials to keep the kits well stocked.
- Front-load your promotion in order to make sure that people know about the kits in a timely manner, and post a few example drawings to pique patrons' (and the staff's) interest. Ellen commented in her feature article that she had great success with one-on-one conversations with people who looked at the example displays, even if they weren't aware of the kits ahead of time.
- Tie in some on-site invitations—if you want. This kind of invitation makes for a great extension to a series of illustration or drawing workshops held by the library. You can promote the kits during applicable workshops, and even have some available for grab-and-go alongside illustration and drawing books.

OFF-SITE INVITATIONS

We really want to encourage library staff to embrace off-site invitations as a key component of the Creative Library. We know that "bodies in the room" is a way to measure success (more on this, and how to go beyond room counts, in chapter 7), but sometimes it's more effective to shake things up a bit by taking the library out and about in the community.

For library staff, especially those with public desk duties or other in-library responsibilities, capacity can be a barrier to planning any off-site activities in addition to what you've already got going on. If you're looking for ways to incorporate some off-site events into your calendar without overextending yourself, here are a couple of ideas:

- Make use of volunteers and interns or fieldwork students. These folks can help pack and unpack off-site activity supplies and even do setup/teardown and help manage a table or booth.
- Train a core group of folks on how to facilitate a project or invitation. For example, the Madison Public Library hosts regular screen-printing

workshops at a variety of community events. This idea originated with the mixed-media artist Craig Grabhorn when he was an artist in residence at The Bubbler. Eventually Craig left Madison, but enough staff had been trained on how to do screen-printing that the in-library and pop-up activities could continue even after the residency had wrapped. Now there's a group of staff who can either help facilitate or train staff at other locations on the process. This relieves any one person from being responsible for every off-site or pop-up screen-printing event.

- Possibly the best option: reverse-pilot an in-library activity that's taking up a lot of your time. We'll go into more details about "reverse-piloting" in chapter 7, but simply put, this means testing *not* doing a series or regular program for a set amount of time (we recommend 3–6 months). During the "reverse pilot" period, do not plan anything new to take that program's place in the library; instead, reach out to an off-site partner you've wanted to work with in the past, and try an off-site pilot.

Off-site invitations can fall under a "placemaking" initiative, which could be part of a larger city endeavor. You can learn more about placemaking examples at the Project for Public Spaces.[8]

Example 1: Drink and Draw

Among the favorite activities organized by The Bubbler at Madison Public Library are the Drink and Draw events that take place a few times a year. These are always held outside of the library at local bars, cafes, or brewing companies.

Drink and Draws are fairly straightforward: library staff show up with a big box of drawing supplies (markers, pencils, pens) and a bunch of half-sheets with drawing prompts written on them. These drawing prompts were the collective brainchild of the poet and art-maker Oliver Bendorf, The Bubbler artist in residence Angela Richardson, and Head Bubblerarian Trent Miller. The prompts offer a starting point for people of any age who might not feel comfortable tackling a drawing project on a blank sheet of paper.

Fig. 3.2 Drawing Prompt Sheet

The prompts range from "draw what you had for breakfast" to "a robot" (shown in figure 3.2) and "a spaceship."

Why we love this project:

- Off-site events like this are one effective way that the library can support neighborhood businesses, by bringing potential customers in and engaging customers in interesting activities. There is no need for this to happen in an establishment that serves alcohol if that's not the vibe you're going for—a coffee shop, outdoor park, or community center works too.
- This project requires only basic setup and supplies on the library's part (the prompts and supplies can be transported in a box or bin).

How you can make this project happen:

- Make a pitch to the business partner before advertising the event in any way. Figure out with them if a set of tables can be reserved for event attendees, and be prepared to make table tents or flyers that can be posted in the establishment.
- If the business partner is amenable, see if it's possible to have a slight discount applied to a beverage if attendees show their library card.
- Don't forget to share drawings! Document both the event and the images for the social media, newsletter, or website.

Example 2: Literary Lots

Literary Lots was a public installation project that took place in Cleveland, Ohio, in 2013–2014. Literary Lots brought to life a number of immersive play structures that were designed to engage the imagination and promote exploration and literacy.

From the Literary Lots website:[9]

> Literary Lots brings magic and the power of imagination to urban kids by turning vacant, underutilized spaces into scenes from children's books. By working with cultural institutions and local non-profits, Literary Lots will not only bring engaging programming to neighborhood kids, but will also provide a transformative experience that combines creative land reuse, artist engagement, youth education, and urban renewal to be enjoyed by all.

By working with artists and engaging partners like the public library and local schools, Literary Lots invited people to take another look and reimagine the possibilities for abandoned city spaces.

The large-scale structures in Literary Lots included spaces that captured moments from *Cloudy with a Chance of Meatballs* (think oversized sandwich "boats" and more) and *Alice in Wonderland* (tea parties, of course).

Why we love this project:

- It's immersive. A project like this embeds literature in the neighborhood beyond the library walls, leaving it open to chance encounters.
- The opportunities for additional invitations abound. Story times, play times, picnics—think of these off-site spaces as extensions of the library building.

How you can make this project happen:

- A full-scale immersive play structure like the ones built for Literary Lots may not be possible. But it is possible to utilize public spaces on a smaller scale. Check out StoryWalk, a project of the Kellogg Hubbard Library,[10] or the Anji Play approach to early learning.[11]
- Think partners, partners, partners: your parks and recreation department, community gardeners, cycling group, farmers market organizers, and placemaking groups or organizations working in urban reclamation. Think outside. Are there already art-makers working with these outdoors partners? What role is possible for the library?

INVITATIONS FOR EXISTING GROUPS

One way to make a big impact with your invitations is to make them available for specific, preexisting groups of people. For example, the Teacher Lab program at the Brooklyn Public Library[12] is an online introduction to library resources and information literacy that is geared toward educators (and it's set up to provide continuing education units for teachers, which is a boon). Is there an opportunity to gear a creative invitation you already have going toward a group like K–12 educators, or community center staff, or even local business owners? We'll expand more on this idea in chapter 4.

WORKING WITH WHAT YOU HAVE ALREADY

There are probably plenty of hands-on invitations already on your event calendar. Before dashing off to add a bunch of new invitations, take a deep breath and examine your calendar to see what's already on there that you could package into a Creative Library platform. Look for things that are designed to foster creativity and hands-on exploration. If you work at a branch of a larger library, it is worthwhile to talk with colleagues at other locations and look at your calendars from a mile-high standpoint. What things are tagged (literally or figuratively) "arts," "creativity," "making," or "hands-on"?

It might make sense to group invitations that already exist under a new umbrella, relating them to one another and encouraging staff and patrons to think about them differently as you incorporate them into your Creative Library platform, rather than (a) starting over from scratch or (b) adding a whole new suite of workshops on top of what you're already doing. (More on this in chapter 9.)

PLANNING NEW INVITATIONS

When it comes to planning new invitations, we've found that it's useful to find a balance between piloting some new ideas to see if they take, and also being responsive to current community needs and wants. It's perfectly reasonable not to have a super-packed invitation calendar if some needs are being met elsewhere, too. Here are some tips for planning and implementing new invitations:

Communicate with other staff. Talk with other programming colleagues to see what creative invitations they've got in the hopper, what's been popular, and who they've been working with to make their invitations happen.

This can be something formal like the Princeton (NJ) Public Library's "programming retreat," which is basically a big workday where programmers get together and collectively plan out a year's worth of events and workshops, or it can be a shared online calendar where staff add their tentative plans and contacts. This communication, whether it's with staff in the same building or at other branches, can be a great way to learn about new partners and facilitators, while also ensuring that you won't accidentally oversaturate the calendar with too many of one kind of workshop or program.

You can incorporate staff who aren't necessarily program planners into the conversation. If you're thinking about marketing creative invitations in a different way or in collaboration with staff in other buildings, you'll absolutely want to loop in your library's marketing staff (if that's not you already) to make sure they're an early part of the branding and platform development—more on this in chapter 9. Talk with collection development folks to get a feel for which arts- and maker-focused titles are experiencing heavy circulation. Are knitting books or origami books getting lots of play at the circulation desk? Offer a short series on the topic to see if hands-on workshops are something patrons are interested in.

Talk with folks who don't work at the library. We'll dive more into this in chapters 4 and 6, but it's important to mention here too. Before sitting back and planning a whole new slate of activities, take some time to talk with folks. Remember the message board activity? Ask a question like "If you could learn any kind of new skill, what would it be?" or "How can [this community] welcome and support artists?" Have conversations with people at the desk. Post a poll on Facebook. Let the library board, the Friends, and other city staff know that you're looking for feedback and ideas.

Commit to diversity and variety when it comes to the kinds of invitations you're offering and the instructors that you're working with.

Consider invitations with a national or local tie-in. Are there events, projects, or campaigns happening at a national level or local level that lend themselves to invitations? The marketing support and the activity ideas that national organizing bodies put together can be a great springboard to incorporate some new invitations into your program calendar without striking out on your own too much. Ideas to look at include the Big Read, the Big Draw, and National Novel Writing Month. On the local level, consider invitations that dovetail with regional festivals or celebrations—a quilting workshop series centered around a local quilting festival, for example. This doesn't necessarily mean planning something for the same weekend as that community celebration, but a few weeks before or after that event can be a good time to try out your invitation.

Balance other community activities. Make sure, before planning anything new, that you have a good sense of what is already happening on a regular basis in your community (check out chapter 4 for more information on the "community survey"). Remember that having fewer, but more series-based and more regular invitations at the library may be more meaningful. And if there's a plethora of computer coding workshops, knitting circles, or pottery classes already happening, *don't plan one!* Instead, pilot one or two new things that fill a want or need (based on your conversations with other staff and community members) and flesh those out with additional offerings if they're successful.

Consider series vs. one-offs. Planning invitations is in large part about balance: balancing off-site invitations with in-house ones; balancing library activities with things that are already happening in the community; and balancing independent invitations with group ones. Whether to plan a series of three invitations or whether to plan one, two, or three one-off invitations is also a question of balance. Overall, we've found that the level of engagement is higher when the learning is scaffolded;[13] that is, when attendees are coming back for multiple workshops that build on knowledge developed in the previous one. You're more likely to achieve that tight-knit group collaborative feel when it's a three-part workshop held over the course of a few weeks.

However, the one-off invitation can serve a different, and also meaningful, role. For example, Laura worked with a community partner to host a Ukulele in Community workshop that ended up having eighty-plus learners working with about thirty ukulele volunteer instructors. The workshop's second part consisted of a giant group "strum-along" with a variety of traditional and contemporary songs displayed on a big screen. The attendees were encouraged to check out future strum-alongs, which take place at various venues around the city. While the library's event was something of a one-off (held annually), it yielded several important outcomes based on reports back from the community partner. Multiple additional workshops were held due to attendance at that initial library activity, and many of the attendees decided to pursue ukulele opportunities elsewhere in town.

A rule of thumb that Laura's team generally applies when planning invitations is to aim for about 70 percent of activities planned in series, with one-offs making up the other 30 percent of invitations. This means that *generally,* we're aiming to plan series of workshops or experiences, but if a fabulous one-off comes along that is just too good to pass up, permission is granted.

We'll drill down on this more in chapter 9, "Packaging and Sharing the Creative Library Platform," but ideally, once you've started packaging and promoting the Creative Library as a platform, those awesome one-offs will actually fit more naturally and be easier to promote as part of a larger, whole-library platform.

Make performances count. Lots of libraries function as venues for performing arts events, from theater performances to puppet shows to different kinds of dance. Exposure to different kinds of performances is certainly important, but let's think about a way to level up from merely watching a performance to engaging with it. Is there an opportunity to integrate a hands-on invitation into the performance?

For example, in 2011 and 2012 the Hedberg Public Library in Janesville, Wisconsin, hosted a very popular and well-attended breakdance competition in partnership with a local dance instructor and studio. Crews from around the upper Midwest showed up to compete, and a lot of people attended that library staff had not seen in the building—or at least at events—before. Prior to the formal competition, the dance studio that helped coordinate the event hosted a workshop for beginners and intermediate breakdancers to learn and polish their skills alongside the more advanced competitors.

In addition to being inspired by the older, more experienced dancers, the (mostly young) people who participated in the hands-on part of the event could in many cases appreciate the competition more because they had just tried out the moves for themselves. This is not unlike a library organizing an author talk or video chat with a teen—or adult—writing group. The questions, and the connection to the performance, are made more meaningful by incorporating an invitation ahead of the performance.

Other ideas along these lines include:

- Hosting a play, staged reading, or other kind of theater performance. Think outside the box when it comes to extensions of the performance you could host. How about an audition workshop for adults (or youth, if that's the target audience for the performance)? If your library has a collection of scripts, librettos, or other materials to support live performance, make a grab-and-go bookmark with information about that collection.
- The same goes for dance performances, or competitions like the breakdancing one mentioned previously. Can you partner with the dance troupe that's coming in, or, to spread the wealth a bit, work with a local studio or instructor in advance of an out-of-town performer visit? See if you can work with them to offer two workshops, broken up either by age or by experience level (beginner/intermediate).
- Incorporating a hands-on component in advance of a music performance may be trickier, given the need for musical instruments. Does your local or regional orchestra have an outreach or community engagement division that could come and do a "petting zoo" with different instruments for patrons of all ages to try? Think about a one-off performance and how it can be expanded into a series of invitations. Not every part of the invitation needs to take place on the same day, or even at the same library branch.

INVITATIONS TAKEAWAYS

1. Invitations, much like your library's collection, should function as windows and mirrors for your community. Windows, so that community members have a chance to learn and try something new; mirrors, so that they see representations of artists from different backgrounds and levels of experience, in a respectful and non-tokenizing way.
2. Do the legwork before planning anything new, both in the library and outside of the library. Talk with your coworkers or staff at neighboring libraries to make sure you know what's going on elsewhere in the organization and regionally. Put the time in to attend community meetings

and meet with a variety of stakeholders to hear ideas and identify gaps or needs/wants that the library, through partnerships and working closely with instructors and facilitators, could fill.

3. Don't be afraid to host library invitations *outside of the library*. And don't be afraid to take a break or "reverse-pilot" an in-house program in order to commit fully to a new off-site one.

4. Aim for an approximately 30 percent–70 percent balance of one-off invitations and series invitations. Embrace the idea of piloting a particular series or new invitation, but make sure you're committing fully for a set amount of time in order to arouse interest and receive feedback on it.

5. Evaluate the platform, and not just new invitations, either. Consider evaluation to be a key part of maintaining the Creative Library platform—apply that lens! Incorporate time for prepping and inputting data from evaluations into your invitation timeline (this may mean you coordinate fewer invitations overall—*that's fine*). There is more on different approaches to evaluating invitations and other facets of the Creative Library in chapter 7.

Notes

1. Suzy Waldo, "Pop des Fleur Winter Pop-up Garden with Carnegie Library of Pittsburgh," 2016, Library as Incubator Project, www.libraryasincubatorproject .org/?p=17841.

2. Adam Atkinson et al., "Kit: Poetry Scavenger Hunt," 2013, Library as Incubator Project, www.libraryasincubatorproject.org/?p=9669.

3. Book to Art Club, www.booktoartclub.squarespace.com.

4. Rachal Duggan, https://www.rachalduggan.com.

5. Eli Rosenberg, "Manhattan Subway Becomes Emotional Outlet after Election," *New York Times*, November 11, 2016, https://www.nytimes.com/2016/11/11/ nyregion/subway-notes-offer-a-form-of-therapy.html.

6. Deanna Dent, "Engage Your Brain on National Puzzle Day," 2018, https:// asunow.asu.edu/20180125-creativity-national-puzzle-day-how-brains-solve.

7. Ellen Paul, "I Draw New London" series, 2012, Library as Incubator Project, www.libraryasincubatorproject.org/?tag=new-london.

8. Project for Public Spaces, "What Is Placemaking?" https://www.pps.org/article/ what-is-placemaking.

9. Literary Lots, http://literarylots.org.

10. Kellogg-Hubbard Library, "StoryWalk," www.kellogghubbard.org/ storywalk.

11. Anji Play, http://www.anjiplay.com/home.

12. Brooklyn Public Library, "Teacher Lab," https://bklynlibrary.teachable.com/p/teacherlab.

13. Rebecca Alber, "6 Scaffolding Strategies to Use with Your Students," updated 2014, *Edutopia* (blog), https://www.edutopia.org/blog/scaffolding-lessons-six-strategies-rebecca-alber.

THE ELEMENTS: PARTNERSHIP AND ENGAGEMENT

NO LIBRARY IS AN ISLAND. INVOLVING—*EMBRACING* PARTNERS, whether they be local educators, facilities or institutions, the businesses around you, or perhaps most importantly, the "everyday" library user—is key to situating the library as an integral part of a vibrant and engaged community. Creative libraries recognize this and find ways to leverage the information and expertise that is held in the backgrounds and experiences of their community partners. Finding access points for partners, and places where those partners can help evaluate and then edit the library's work, ensures that the invitations from the library are meaningful for its immediate community.

At the very least, partnerships ensure that responsibility is distributed and that the library can simply do more with limited staff time and resources. For example, when Laura was about to leave her position as a solo youth librarian at a small-town library for impending maternity leave, she made sure that every school-age and family program that season (except for story times, which would be covered in-house) had a committed, external partner co-leading the activity, so that the show could go on even if Laura had to bow out early or altogether.

Pretty much every library works with a partner in some capacity already—the local elementary school, the senior center, or the local chamber of commerce. What we're going to examine in this chapter is partnerships with the Creative Library platform in mind, and consequently, many of the example partners that we discuss will be arts-related in some way. But this idea applies to any kind of "platform" you're interested in cultivating, and it can help you develop that platform faster and more effectively.

In this chapter, we will mainly focus on *external* partners and engagement. Check out chapter 5 for ideas related to partnering with and engaging internal staff in the Creative Library platform.

THE COMMUNITY SURVEY

Let's assume that you're interested in connecting with potential partners in your community who can help cultivate a Creative Library platform. The first step we suggest is to start "surveying" your community—this is not taking an evaluative survey for feedback, but doing the work of a surveyor to take a broad look at your community. You may have heard of "asset mapping" in the framework of asset-based community development.[1] This is a similar idea. Where are the folks who are already engaged in creative work or in providing creative programs for the public?

These could be formal institutions like art museums, colleges, or universities; neighborhood hubs like community centers; businesses like art supply shops and galleries; or independent artists and creatives. Glean what you can from websites, social media profiles, and the like, but if possible, reach out for a short phone conversation or an in-person get-together to find out more about the organization's or individual's mission and goals, the kinds of resources they offer, and if these cost anything.

The community survey is useful on a number of fronts:

1. You lessen the risk of duplicating efforts—which is particularly important if you're in a small town or neighborhood. We touched on this in chapter 2: a good example of this came up when the staff who would eventually develop The Bubbler at Madison Public Library were having preliminary conversations with other arts and maker organizations in Madison to determine where the gaps were in creative outlets and resources for adults, and what role the library could play in that area. There had already been plans for a digital media lab in the new Central Library building. Should that be expanded, to go beyond access to software and audio and video engineering equipment to include heavy-duty equipment like power tools, soldering irons, and the like? What about the seemingly ubiquitous 3D printer? Conversations with local makerspaces helped guide the folks who were working on The Bubbler concept away from going all-in on specialized tools and equipment—in Madison, there were already several places where people could get access to them, and

under the guidance of much more experienced educators. Rather than take an inch-deep/mile-wide approach, which dilutes the quality of the programming, The Bubbler team chose to dive deep in response to what people demonstrated an interest in.

2. It's best to build support and establish community ownership over the Creative Library platform early, rather than trying to entice people after the fact. By doing a "community survey" you will likely discover or rediscover places and people that are doing work which is adjacent to the library's work. You may not have realized that the neighborhood center down the road also has an art gallery space and may be interested in working with you to host Book to Art Club meetings. Or that the local theater guild runs free audition workshops and would like to expand these to reach a new group of potential cast members.

3. You should figure out what people want in an organic, not forced, way. Take the example of the screen-printing workshops at the Madison Public Library. The artist in residence Craig Grabhorn facilitated screen-printing stations at a number of library and other community locations, and the community response was overwhelming. It turns out that people *love* screen-printing. Now there are a handful of library staff both in and beyond The Bubbler core team who are trained to facilitate the screen-printing activities, thereby making these activities much more sustainable than they would be if the library relied solely on a temporary artist in residence to run them. And The Bubbler Room at the Central Library, which is essentially a blank space with tables, chairs, and a standard sink, now has a permanent screen-printing sink installed in a corner, a testament to the staying power and community interest in that particular activity. Had The Bubbler staff not done the work of finding out where the opportunities were already, and taken their time when determining what equipment to purchase, they might well have ended up duplicating another organization's services and missed out on a chance to be truly community-driven in their decision-making.

THE COMMUNITY SURVEY HOW-TO

1. When conducting a community survey, start by making a list of potential partners in the community. It's easy to begin with those arts partners the library already works with, but don't limit yourself to only these organi-

zations or individuals. Poke around online, look on Facebook, and always ask the question: "Who else should we talk to?" Ask library colleagues in your area who they're working with—and not just colleagues in like institutions, either; if you work in a public library, make sure you're talking with academic librarians and school librarians as well. Check out meet-up groups that focus on creativity or the arts.

2. Remember that it's okay to weed out some potential partners right away. As you're working on your list, you might realize that there are just too many organizations to tackle every single group that could fall under the "arts and creativity" umbrella. It's perfectly reasonable to dive in deeper on visual arts, or performing arts, or writers and writing groups. If you start with one creative segment of the community, it'll be easier to replicate a similar approach with another segment later. If your list feels reasonable and includes potential partners from a wide variety of creativity and arts fields, that's great too.

3. Meet with people on the phone or in person when you can. E-mail is okay, but a conversation on the phone or in person can ultimately take less time, and makes for a more meaningful connection right away.

4. Take your time, but make time for it. As we all know, library work waxes and wanes depending on the time of year and staff capacity. There's no rush on completing the community survey. However, we do encourage you to set aside time to focus on the community survey and the subsequent phone or in-person meetings. When thinking about time management in this way, it can be useful to think about this process as similar to the collection development of library materials—setting aside time to read reviews, determine purchases, manage relationships with vendors, and the like. There's no magic number of hours that you "should" spend on this. Can you spare a half-day per week? You have permission not to have an overpopulated programming or invitation calendar, and to "reverse-pilot" some programs in order to free up time and head-space in order to dive deeper on community engagement.

5. Listen and learn. Each meeting with a potential partner will look and feel a little bit different depending on that partner's prior relationship to the library. For an initial meeting, keeping the "agenda" very broad is often a good thing because it keeps you from making assumptions about if and how the potential partner may want to interface with the library and the Creative Library platform. You're not the expert here; they are. Instead of diving right in to the details of what the library is planning and pitch-

ing a bunch of collaboration ideas, "zoom out" first and ask for a broader view of what the individual or organization does, where they fit in the grand scheme of arts and creative resources in the community, and what, if any, gaps they see in resources for local artists and makers. If there's something tangible to offer up in the moment, go for it, but treat this as more of a fact-finding and brainstorming session than a pitch.

6. Offer to follow up. Ask if they're interested in staying apprised of the progress on this platform. Depending on their time and interest, opportunities for follow-up range from an e-mail list with updates to more in-depth collaboration and involvement in the planning process.

COMMUNITY ENGAGEMENT AND THE CREATIVE LIBRARY

As more and more libraries invest in engagement, outreach, and partnership-oriented staff positions, we definitely want to talk about the importance of community engagement and ownership in the Creative Library platform.[2] There's going to be a bit of a push-pull here, because while we're talking about community engagement, we're simultaneously championing gathering those resources that already exist under the Creative Library's "umbrella." But as the platform develops, changes, expands, and refocuses (a multiyear process), we strongly encourage that it continue to be informed and driven by community members. This means involving folks who are not library staff not only as feedback providers, but also as planners and budget advisors, and it means providing formalized opportunities for people to engage deeply with the platform for their own ends and for their own priorities and projects. Check out chapter 6, "The Lenses: Community-Led Invitations," for some actionable ideas in this regard. In the second half of this chapter, we will examine what partnerships with different kinds of groups (rather than individual community members) might look like as these relate to the Creative Library platform. This will look different for each library and each community, so feel free to take tidbits from this section and apply them in whatever way makes sense for your library.

Working with Organizations

There are a number of ways that organizations can end up interfacing with the Creative Library platform. First, let's define what we mean by *organization*. We're thinking about a group of people who are affiliated around a specific mission (e.g., a nonprofit group working with people who are experiencing homelessness), profession (a teachers' association), or an interest or hobby (independent filmmakers, playwrights). The ways you work with different organizations or kinds of organizations will vary, and you'll leverage the people power behind these organizations at different times to different ends.

Here are some ideas:

> Collaborate with an arts organization on an invitation or series of invitations (something you may already be doing). As noted in chapter 3, working collaboratively with individual artists or a group of artists not only levels up the kind of invitation you can offer, but also offers a chance to expand your reach when it comes to marketing and promoting the invitation.

> In the Pop de Fleurs invitation example, the library worked closely with a local fiber arts guild to make a series of drop-in invitations happen, not to mention the community art installation at the end of it all.

> The Music Lab at the Public Library of Cincinnati and Hamilton County is an invitation that is the product of a partnership between the library and *two* local orchestras: the Cincinnati Symphony Orchestra and the Cincinnati Pops Orchestra. Musicians from the orchestras come to the library (usually as part of a larger arts program or event), and kids and families have the opportunity to hear musical instruments being played, experiment with an instrument, and interact with real classical musicians.[3]

> Even when you are not the "programmer" or invitation facilitator, there's a lot of work involved when it comes to partnering with organizations. Communication is usually spotty (probably on both ends—everyone's got a lot going on), and it can be hard to even find a time to meet in person. This is one reason why the community survey work is so handy to do ahead of time. When you put in the work to track people down and talk to them first without an agenda or a specific request, it's a lot easier to pick up the communication again when it comes time to propose a collaborative invitation. Plus, those organizations will already have some idea of what you're talking about instead of your having to introduce yourself, the library, the platform you're developing, *and* make the ask. Whether you officially contract with the organization depends on your library's typical practice, but at the very least, plan on

writing up and agreeing upon a set of expectations so that everyone is clear about what's expected.

Hold a community conversation forum. Make yourself available to attend an organization meeting in order to have a conversation about the Creative Library platform. Sometimes an organization's representative may pitch this to you, but if they don't, make the offer to come to them (or to host them at the library) in order to talk with and hear from the organization's members directly.

As usual, it's best to do this as you're developing the platform, so that you're incorporating ideas right off the bat. And yes, it takes a significant amount of time to go out and meet with folks. Plan accordingly. Talk with your supervisor ahead of time and figure out how this will work with work schedules and hour allotments so that you're not working for free. Offer to host the organization's next meeting at the library if you can't go to them. If groups typically have to pay to use library meeting rooms, see if you can cut them a break for accommodating your limited capacity.

A tip for these conversations: similar rules apply as with the community survey. Use the "zoom out" approach and focus more on how the entire community or neighborhood can be more welcoming or friendly for creatives, rather than drilling down on the details of what the library specifically can (or can't) do. As people raise ideas and suggestions, others can offer up ideas about resources that may already exist, or you can do a little connecting after the fact if you know of a place in town that already offers coworking spaces or a toolshare or tool library.

Target organizations by offering them hands-on invitation opportunities. If you're looking to get away from the "throw it at the wall and see what sticks" approach to workshops and other invitations, try taking a step back. Instead of planning a roster of workshops that people may or may not show up for, is there a way that you can pilot a "workshop on demand" where organizations can place a request for a specific workshop topic for a certain number of people? If you have a digital media lab or makerspace that experiences downtime during the school or work day, this may be a chance to invite a new audience into the library and help local organizations build capacity.

One extremely successful example of a library working closely with a specific, targeted audience whose members have professional development opportunities is that of the Teacher Lab at the Brooklyn Public Library. This online (read: *flexible*), unlimited enrollment course in information literacy skills fulfills a number of the continuing education credit hours that K–12 educators need to maintain their certification in New York. It might be worth exploring with your school district to see what would be necessary for library workshops to fulfill professional development or continuing education requirements for teachers. If it's a matter of expanding one aspect of a workshop or series that you already do, why not pilot it for a year?

The chances are very good that you've already got solid relationships with a lot of organizations in your community or region. The ideas above may make sense for you, or you may need to go in a different direction. In any case, it's worth thinking about the different possibilities for organizational involvement with the Creative Library platform, and taking enough time to flesh out the ideas and document them in an organized way (see chapter 9 for more on this).

Working with Individual Artists and Other Makers

In addition to working with organizations and other groups, you'll likely be working with individual artists (who may be part of an organization or collective, but are flying solo when it comes to interfacing with the library) on a regular basis. There are a number of different ways that individuals can inform and make up the Creative Library platform, with some special considerations that you'll want to think about and plan for in advance.

Here are some ideas:

The community survey work very much applies to these folks. As working and/or practicing artists, these people will play an important and multifaceted role in the Creative Library platform. You'll want to hear from them as much as possible before getting too deep in the development or expansion of Creative Library resources. How do they use the library in their work now? What's missing in the way of resources, for them, in the community as it stands right now? Who's doing really interesting work in the arts community? And vitally: who else should you be talking to? Be prepared for a variety of responses. Make sure to ask folks if they'd like to be included on follow-up communications, and send them a thank-you for their time.

You may end up asking some of these individuals to facilitate a creative invitation at the library. This seems like a good time to bring up an important point: the question of whether you should pay your facilitators or not. As librarians, we totally understand that you're likely working with a shoestring budget for invitations. On the other hand, it's *really* important not to expect that facilitators will be able to work for free for the library. If you can offer *something,* do so—and if supplies come from a different budget line, please offer to cover the cost of materials for the invitation. If this means you do less invitations overall, *that's fine.* It's better to invest in a few meaningful invitations than in a bunch of them that rely on volunteer labor, from both a practical *and* a philosophical standpoint.

There will also be individuals who reach out to *you* to offer their time and expertise as a facilitator or instructor for a workshop or other invitation. Remember, you don't need to say "yes" to hosting every pitch that comes your way, especially if you're at risk of "mission creep," where the lens for the Creative Library platform expands and expands until it's unwieldy or meaningless. Invitations, as noted in chapter 3, should be curated as carefully as the materials on the shelves, even if the person making the pitch is willing to volunteer his or her time. Take some time to consider how you evaluate invitation ideas (see chapter 9 for helpful policies and practices) and then make it really easy for people to fill out a form with their idea (the staff can also help people fill it out in person or over the phone).[4]

One resource that the staff at The Bubbler at Madison Public Library created fairly early on is the Teaching Artist Database.[5] This is a database powered by AirTable that includes short entries about each artist with their biography, the media they work in, the age group they're interested in working with, their contact information, and a quick description of their involvement with The Bubbler. This is a great resource for schools, community and neighborhood centers, senior centers, and even neighboring libraries that would like to work with these artists, and it is a tangible way to support the local artists that the library works with.

No matter how awesome or useful, projects or resources like the Teaching Artist Database can devour one's time and effort. When it's a matter of doing a bunch of information-gathering—for example, communicating with the artists you've worked with to ask if they'd like to be included in a database and then collecting and inputting each person's information—it might be worth asking an intern, fieldwork student, or a committed project-based volunteer to do much of the information-collecting and maintenance once the database has been assembled. And if there's just not a lot of interest from artists, or if you're finding you have to pull teeth in order to get the database entries populated, the project is probably just not worth the time. If your community or county already has a teaching artist database or directory, it's better to be aware of it and be able to refer people to it.

For those folks who might be too busy or are not comfortable with teaching or facilitating an invitation, is there an opportunity to engage them in a different way, maybe with a short "what are you working on right now" Q&A, or asking them to provide a "recommended reads" list for people who are interested in the medium they work in? In addition to creating a channel for the community to learn about these artists' processes and practices, you can also do a little shelf-checking for yourself or your library's collection development staff—what's available in the library, what isn't, and can you get it?

Don't neglect the performers! (Especially if you're including performing arts in the Creative Library platform.) Finished performances are not the only way that performing artists can be involved with the Creative Library. Do you have space for table readings, rehearsals, and auditions? Is there an opportunity for an audition workshop, or an acting resume workshop or review, and can the library and a local theater group cosponsor a day of free headshots?

Individuals working in creative fields are frequently professional, full-time artists and makers, but they're also looking for professional development opportunities in order to expand their skill sets. The Work of Art workshop series at the Hennepin County Library in Minneapolis offered artists a chance to explore topics ranging from "Career Planning for Artists" to "Time Management for Artists," "Small Business Planning for Artists," and many more. During your community survey phase, it might be worth asking what resources already exist in the community to support the professional aspects of being a working artist. You may discover a gap, and there may be an opportunity to work with these folks to fill it in.

There are so many possibilities for individual artists to drive the development of the Creative Library. Exactly what these will look like depends on a range of external factors, and don't worry if it takes a little while to find a good rhythm.

Working with Other Institutions

Institutions nearby could include K–12 schools, community colleges, universities, museums, local theaters or performing arts centers, and even other libraries. Institutional engagement with the Creative Library can happen at various points in the platform's development and will create a richer platform overall.

Here are some ideas:

Include the institutions' staff—and their students—in your community survey. If you work at a public library, reach out to a studio art class at the local high school or college to talk with faculty and students about the resources they're interested in, what's missing from the landscape locally, what makes a great arts community, and more. When working with youth on something like this, make sure your youth services folks are looped in; they may even be interested in helping to facilitate this kind of conversation.

Making sure that institutions are helping to drive the process early on means that they're less likely to feel that the library is stepping on their toes, intentionally or unintentionally. You can help assuage their concerns (that you're duplicating their own programs) by having these conversations early in the process, and stressing that the goal is really to fill in gaps in local resources (if possible). If you don't already have a contact who can connect you with the best person in an institution, try searching for a community engagement coordinator, public education coordinator, or someone else on the staff with an outward-facing position title.

Always ask the question of who else you should talk to; institutions typically also work with unaffiliated artists who may not be officially on their staff, but who would be good connections for you to have.

Take the library to these institutions. Remember that invitations can happen anywhere, not just in the library building. A great example of this is partnering with an art museum or art center on a Book to Art Club, where the library brings the book discussion facilitation expertise and the museum or center brings the hands-on project expertise. Make sure you come to an agreement ahead of time about how to make this a free program—can the library cover or split the cost of project supplies, for example? Get a feel for the institution's invitation schedule. Do they have a monthly or seasonal event where the library could be a cohost?

Think about what's in it for the institution. Is there an engagement or partnership opportunity that takes advantage of what you already have available in the library? Professors and instructors might be interested in an assignment or project that allows their students to engage directly and deeply with library materials. You never know what kinds of things people are interested in, but it's absolutely worth an invitation to say: "here are some interesting collections we have," or "here's the different spaces that you and your students can engage with," and then see what people come up with. There are some really terrific "real world" examples of projects like this to explore.

In 2013 staff from the Edinburgh Central Library, in partnership with faculty from the Edinburgh College of Art, invited art students into the library to plumb the depths of the library's distinctive collections in order to gather inspiration for new works.[6] Once installed adjacent to the library's physical collections, these new works formed an Interactive Art Trail, leading visitors through the library to explore often overlooked collections in a new, highly visual way.

In 2018, the University of Wisconsin–Milwaukee Libraries found a new way to highlight their digital collections and develop a relationship with local artists through their "Look Here!" pilot project.[7] Artists were invited to explore the libraries' numerous digital collections to find inspiration for new work, and they talked with librarians to get a rundown of fair use rules and how they applied to creative work. The artists' finished works were installed at a nearby art museum for the public to view, making it a collaborative project across cultural institutions. Adjacent projects included a series of interviews with participating artists, which was published on the university libraries' blog.

Part of the magic in the two above examples comes from an open invitation to explore the library's collections. There's a willingness and excitement on the part of these libraries to go with the flow and work with the artists to make sure they had what they needed in order to produce new works.

When in doubt, get back to basics. It could be that what the institution you're working with *really* wants is some traditional library services, or just to know what's going on. Does your local high school performing arts faculty know that they, or their students, can check out books of audition monologues, play scripts, and music scores? Does your neighborhood art center know that they can refer students for research help or to obtain visual arts encyclopedias for reference? Is your local art museum aware of your small but lively gallery space, and can you help cross-promote each other's exhibitions? Does the local theater company know that they can reserve library meeting rooms for table reads or auditions? Sometimes people just want to know where to refer people, and having at least a check-in from the public library every year or so helps keep those resources on people's radar—plus, you establish connections and can tap into them when there's an opportunity to organize something on a larger scale.

Spend some time with an institution's community-based learning staff. This is especially pertinent when it comes to colleges and universities. Academic institutions are often looking for community-based learning or service learning opportunities in which their faculty and students can work with a community partner, usually on a particular project or topic with deep engagement and reflection built in to the curriculum. Is there a project within the Creative Library platform that might be a good fit for a group of students to work on? Ask the community-based learning office for examples of previous projects that have worked well, and meet with them in person to discuss any ideas you have before committing to anything formal.

Partnering and engaging institutions in your community may seem to be a no-brainer, but as with any relationship, challenges and barriers may come up around mission, funding, or lack of communication on one end or the other. The library must be open to new approaches and ideas, but it must also maintain reasonable boundaries and expectations, so it's okay if it takes a while to get something new under way.

Working with Local Businesses

As with the previous examples, your library may already work with local businesses in some capacity. When Laura was a youth services librarian, much of every spring was spent writing letters to businesses asking for their support of the library's summer reading program. With a limited programming budget, that support was vital to plan invitations for kids. Are there ways to go a step further, beyond an annual check-in and request for donations, when working with local businesses, particularly in supporting the Creative Library?

Here are some ideas:

Take the library to these businesses. We discussed this in chapter 3 when talking about off-site invitations, but what we said there bears repeating: not all library activities have to occur in the library. Whether it's a Book to Art Club that meets in a nearby coffeehouse, a Drink and Draw at local bars or restaurants, or something else, many businesses will appreciate the potential for extra traffic. See if they can provide coupons or a free first beverage to invitation participants. Travel to different businesses to ensure you're not playing favorites.

Include small businesses in your community survey. This is a natural fit for businesses that revolve around arts and creativity (art supply stores, bookstores, fabric shops, art galleries), but other businesses may also have interesting ideas or creativity-related events and resources that you'll want to be aware of. Coffee shops or restaurants may feature local artists' work, and of course, open mic nights and music performances can take place at any number of venues.

Talking with many different kinds of business owners and staff about their hopes and goals for the arts community in your town or neighborhood may yield some interesting perspectives. See if you can reach a number of people at the same time by visiting a small business owner gathering or meet-up, and then offer to meet one-on-one with individuals at a later time if people are interested. Sometimes just by showing up and listening, you can pick up on trends and ideas that may not come out in other forums.

You can partner with a business on hosting a program series. You may end up with a business that's interested in either sponsoring or facilitating a series of invitations. As with any facilitator or sponsor, you'll want to be clear about the expectations on both sides. If the business will pay facilitators directly, that's great—otherwise you may need to involve your foundation or Friends group if the businesses involved will be making a large monetary donation to support a program.

You can create a wish list for equipment or supplies. Once you've talked with people and observed what kinds of invitations folks are interested in, there may come a point when you're in need of some equipment or supplies to support the projects people want to do. If businesses ask how they can help out, include a wish list of equipment (sewing machines, iPads, screens for screen-printing) or supplies and ask businesses to donate enough to get you through a year of invitations.

Try to create meaningful volunteer opportunities. Many companies have social responsibility programs in which employees are encouraged or required to engage in volunteer work of some kind. Let these folks know that you're open to being a partner for this kind of program, and have a conversation with them ahead of time to find out what kind of skills and interest people from the company are bringing to the table. Professional project managers, for example, may be able to help the library do some project planning—plotting out a plan to do a podcast, or even helping to develop a web portal for the Creative Library. Make sure to credit these folks when projects go live, and if you feel comfortable, offer to write a letter of recommendation about their volunteer work.

Businesses are an important part of a dynamic community, and there will always be folks who are excited to work with the library. Make sure you know your library's guidelines about promoting businesses or services in town and what the library can and can't do. Clear communication and expectation-setting are key.

PARTNERSHIPS AND ENGAGEMENT TAKEAWAYS

• Don't underestimate the importance of keeping track of partners and contacts, particularly if you're part of a big library with multiple locations and multiple people working on similar projects. Whether you use a project management software, or a spreadsheet with partner information and a primary contact person, there should be some system in place that everyone is aware of and knows how to use, when to update it, and so on. This enables you to know across departments who has already been contacted about what, so that you can avoid over-asking for people's time and/or resources.

- Keep in mind that time is a vital resource and people have limited quantities of it. Make sure that you're not just asking the same people (no matter how amazing) for their time over and over again, whether it's as a program facilitator or as someone who's helping connect the library with the community. This is something to especially be aware of if you are a person with privilege asking for time from people with less privilege. We highly recommend taking a look at the online article "Are You or Your Org Guilty of Trickle-Down Community Engagement" by Vu Le[8] to check your process and make sure that you're not employing people of color, people with disabilities, and people representing other underserved groups to do engagement work or provide input for you for little or no monetary compensation. We'll speak about this more in chapter 6.

How you partner with and engage with entities in your community will be very specific to you, your library, and the people whom you work with now or could work with in the future. Keep an open mind about what partnerships could look like, but be ready with some possibilities if people ask. People's capacity will change, and don't take it personally if someone is not in a position to work with the library at the moment.

Notes

1. ABCD Institute, "Resources," https://resources.depaul.edu/abcd-institute/resources/Pages/default.aspx.

2. Tim Moore et al., "Community Engagement: A Key Strategy for Improving Outcomes for Australian Families," Australian Institute of Family Studies, 2016, https://aifs.gov.au/cfca/publications/community-engagement.

3. Laura Damon-Moore, "Music Lab at the Public Library of Cincinnati and Hamilton County," 2017, Library as Incubator Project, www.libraryasincubatorproject.org/?p=19462.

4. Madison Public Library, "Library Programming Application," https://www.madisonpubliclibrary.org/events/library-programming-application.

5. The Bubbler at Madison Public Library, "Teaching Artist Database," http://madisonbubbler.org/teaching-artist-database/.

6. Laura Damon-Moore, "Interactive Art Trail at Edinburgh Central Library," 2013, Library as Incubator Project, www.libraryasincubatorproject.org/?p=11753.

7. UW-Milwaukee Digital Collections, "Look Here" series, https://uwmdigital collections.blogspot.com/search/label/Look%20Here%21%20project.

8. Vu Le, "Are You or Your Org Guilty of Trickle-Down Community Engagement?" 2015, http://tsne.org/blog/are-you-or-your-org-guilty-trickle-down-community -engagement.

5

THE ELEMENTS: LIBRARY STAFF

ONE OF THE MOST SIGNIFICANT RESOURCES YOU CAN leverage in the Creative Library isn't something you have to write a grant for, or something you have to put on your to-buy list. It's not customizable space, or computer programs, or even a fantastic partner workshop series that brings different arms of the community together to, say, yarn-bomb the entire neighborhood in the dead of winter.

No, the most bottomless resource the creative library has is *its own people*. After all, someone in the library has to say *yes* when the fiber arts guild proposes a yarn-bombing event—and then help organize the thing! People with energy and ideas and passions—these folks are already on your staff, and are ready and willing to lend their enthusiasm and expertise to projects under that "other duties as assigned" header, if only they're given the right climate and opportunity. In fact, they may be *dying* to do just that. There is quite a lot of grunt work in library land: basic transactions at the checkout desk, stickering new books, unloading holds deliveries from other libraries, and shelving. And if your role is primarily on the front lines and at the front desk, if you're not involved in any planning or purchasing, it can be easy to feel like you don't matter.

The truth is, the library is a microcosm of the community. The same goals we have for our cities and towns are mirrored in the goals we aspire to within the library: all of us are gathered around the ongoing project of enriching people's lives, supporting their individual goals by connecting them with information, and giving them space to learn and explore—for free.

Staff support for the creative library is something you can build by inviting staff to share their creativity and passions. We saw successful examples of this at many libraries that shared their stories on the Library as Incubator Project website, with approaches ranging from straightforward opportunities for staff to lend particular expertise to materials selection or program development, to massive community-driven projects, and even to library-sponsored staff retreats like the paid staff artist residency we talked about in chapter 2, where staff are recognized as artists and their contributions are integral to surfacing the library's collections.

In this chapter, we'll look more closely at some exciting methods that libraries have found to showcase the extra-library talents of their staff, enabling them to contribute to their workplace and their community in creative ways, and we'll show how you can build that kind of trust and professional support with your own staff. At the end of the chapter, we'll share some exercises and ideas for growing a Creative Library mindset, from onboarding new employees to high-level planning and service ownership by more experienced staff.

HANDMADE CRAFTERNOONS AT THE NEW YORK PUBLIC LIBRARY

Jessica Pigza[1] is a librarian, an avid seamstress and knitter, and an enthusiast of books and other objects that you can learn to make by hand. She's also a reluctant phenom among rare books librarians, and we had the pleasure of working with her on several Library as Incubator projects, both online and in person. Jessica is now the outreach and exhibits librarian for special collections and archives at the McHenry Library at the University of California–Santa Cruz, but when we met her she worked in the Rare Books Division of the New York Public Library in a variety of roles, including assistant curator of rare books, where she originated the popular Handmade Crafternoon program series. Here, we share an excerpt from her original post from several years ago on the Library as Incubator Project website, in which she told us how she created the Handmade Crafternoons series to make the NYPL's special collections accessible:

Today, Handmade Crafternoons are well established at the New York Public Library and have achieved both momentum and support. But in early 2009, it was just a kernel of an idea. My colleagues and I had just wrapped up Design by the Book, a video series celebrating the possibilities for design inspiration at the library. I wanted to build on this theme and introduce a larger community of creative makers to the collections, and I decided that an ongoing do-it-yourself salon for adults would be the way to do it.

To launch the series, I collaborated with Maura Madden, who is a big supporter of libraries, a craft-loving comedy writer, and the author of an inspiring book called *Crafternoon*. Although every event in the series is a little different, each is built around a few common elements: a visiting special guest artist or maker, a hands-on project, and an intriguing selection of books and magazines from the library's collection. I make these books available for browsing during the event, and I aim for a variety of contemporary and vintage offerings in order to demonstrate the range of materials the library has to offer.

Handmade Crafternoons occur monthly on Saturday afternoons in the spring and fall. They are free, and although we provide as many supplies as possible for each project, we sometimes ask for attendees to bring things as well. After the special guest speaks for a few minutes about their creative work, the rest of the two hours are spent in making, sharing, browsing, and talking. There's often a choose-your-own-craft-adventure vibe to the event, since crafters move at their own speeds, and each person's creation is a unique riff on the day's project. We've made zines, learned about lace, made felt finger puppets, explored slow fashion, done embroidery and fabric stamping, created pop-up books, made little walnut shell boats, and more.

After three years, the series still succeeds at drawing in curious creatives and introducing potential users to the library's collections. Although I can't measure how many new library users have resulted from my outreach efforts, I continue to be heartened when newcomers tell me how Handmade Crafternoon's relaxed social environment made them feel welcome and comfortable in a building that can seem intimidating at times.

Handmade Crafternoons may not be lush and polished theater, but neither are they dry instruction classes either. They live in a happy middle ground where users discover what the library can offer in a welcoming environment. Although Handmade Crafternoons began as an experiment, the series has now earned support from both colleagues and the administration, who are appreciative of its informal and innovative outreach. I'm proud to support the library's mission through my efforts, and I am incredibly grateful that my work has inspired other librarians to encourage new users and new uses for their unique collections.

—Jessica Pigza

Jessica's work to connect people with interesting historical resources and ephemera as inspiration for handmade crafts also informed her book *Bibliocraft: A Modern Crafter's Guide to Using Library Resources to Jumpstart Creative Projects* (2014), which combines her two loves—libraries and handmade design projects. In it, she provides readers with the skills and the inspiration to uncover fresh design ideas among the unique, historical, and unusual collections in libraries worldwide. The book is a real gem, but it also shows how Jessica's personal love of crafting and handmade items informs her professional work. She loves the collections she works with as a librarian so much that she wants to share them with anyone who will listen and stitch along with her, thereby creating a vital outreach opportunity and surfacing collections that are often the most closely guarded and hardest to find, especially in an institution as large as the NYPL.

ADULT DAY CAMP AT THE DARIEN LIBRARY

We love Mallory Arents at the Darien Library in Connecticut, and not just because she is a brilliant programming librarian. It's because she got into libraries because she loves *people*. Her astute empathy for and delight in the people around her—their excitement over *Hamilton,* or their anxiety about trying online dating later in life—mean that she can think critically about the *experiences* her programs create for the folks who attend.

This quality is especially potent when she brings her own experiences and passions to the table—her love of Korean food, K-Pop, and geeky summer camp fun, for instance, and her experience of being a young professional living far from home (she's a Florida native) and working in a community that is geared to families with parents who commute to New York City each day. Mallory had her own struggle to find her community when she first took on a role at Darien, so when she and her programming colleagues were trying to think of ways to draw in the elusive twenties and thirties set (the white whale of programming), she had a deeper perspective to bring to the table.

The result was a series called Adult Day Camp, and we interviewed Mallory about it to learn more.

Library as Incubator Project (LAIP): Tell us about Adult Day Camp. Who is the target audience, and what kinds of activities are in the mix?

Mallory: Adult Day Camp is a series of events meant to attract young professionals. All of our events riff off the idea of summer camp and nostalgia—we host Slime Labs, Nerf Blaster Capture the Flag, a young adult book group, and Awful Movie Night, to name just a few.

What we heard time and time again from this audience is that they were looking for two things:

1. A space to meet people (noting how difficult it is to make friends after college)
2. Something to do outside of the happy hour scene

Our greatest success is always after the events happen: when attendees linger, discussing where they're going to get dinner together, or plan their next time out with one another. I'm proud to say that several dates have even happened as a result of our series!

LAIP: Can you tell us a little bit about how Adult Day Camp got started?

Mallory: Adult Day Camp was born at our Annual Staff Day in 2015. When we asked our entire staff to identify unmet community needs, they saw that we were missing the young professional set. The economy was still reeling from the Great Recession, and we noticed an increase in young professionals moving back home to live with their parents, or moving to a brand-new place for a new job. We wanted to capture this group and make them active library users.

LAIP: How did you get the word out once Adult Day Camp was a thing?

Mallory: The series is marketed solely through the Meetup online service. (Try as we might, twenty-year-olds will never check our library's website to find out what is happening on a Friday night.) We're about three years old now with over 2,500 members. Using Meetup has allowed us to attract an entirely new audience, one that our staff knew was out there, but which we were having a difficult time snagging.

In addition to using Meetup, we also actually disguise the fact that a library is behind all the fun. Twenty- and thirty-somethings have an idea in their minds about what is possible at a public library, and honestly, this viewpoint is often limiting. Our first step is to get people to attend an event, and from then on they're hit over the head with the fact that a library is making it all possible!

LAIP: What were some of the challenges you faced in experimenting with this kind of programming?

Mallory: This series of events has allowed our team to experiment in all of the best ways—our audience expects things a little outside of the box! Some of the best ideas for events have come from our non-programming staff, and I've loved their enthusiasm. The Stained Glass workshop, a Taste Test of weird chips and soda, and Field Day were all suggested by other staff members, and this is a real testament to their confidence in our ability to support young professionals through public programming. I'd love to be more intentional about encouraging the rest of our staff to generate ideas.

LAIP: What's your favorite thing about Adult Day Camp?

Mallory: Time and time again, I've received wonderful comments about how participants can't believe you could do "this" in a Library. One of our regulars even wrote a touching Medium article[2] about what the series has meant to him. Meetup has allowed us to cleverly disguise some of the great events we were already hosting: they're just in a new package for a new audience. We haven't just brought in a new group of library users, we've brought in a new group of "super" library users. These folks aren't just attending events passively, they're talking about it on Twitter and Instagram. They're bringing their friends by. And they're asking if they can donate the few extra bucks they have to our cause.

....

What's so compelling about Mallory's story and Adult Day Camp is the focus on community-building—Adult Day Camp is meant to create a third place for an unmoored group of people, and to make that place the library (as an organization to "belong" to and then as a building). If someone on your staff says they got into libraries because they love learning and the wealth of free access to knowledge was inspiring, that's great. But if someone says they got into libraries because they love *people*, they might be a connector the way Mallory is. It's important to nurture staff who approach the institution of the library in a different way—because their perspective and approach can make it more than it already is, one personal connection (or Nerf Blaster) at a time.

EXPERIMENTAL MUSIC
AT THE CINCINNATI PUBLIC LIBRARY

Steve Kemple served as a music reference librarian at the Cincinnati Public Library for many years, and in between the usual pop, classical, and hip-hop offerings he collected, he found ways to inject his own personal passion into his job through programming. One of his primary obscure interests is experimental music, which he defines this way:

> Experimental music is a way of composing sounds using nonstandard musical instruments (or standard musical instruments in nonstandard ways). Circuit bending, for example, is a common aspect of experimental music pieces—it's the process of modifying ("bending") the circuitry of small electrical devices, often old toys, to produce sounds they weren't otherwise intended to make. John Cage was an influential American composer and music theorist who pioneered many of the ideas and techniques of experimental music.

So, this is not exactly mainstream fare, even in Cincinnati, which has some claim to fame in the experimental music world as the birthplace of a technique called circuit bending. And yet, when Steve launched Experimental Music at the Library in the summer of 2012 . . . it took off. Every other Wednesday, Steve and his team invited a different experimental act to perform in the Popular Library Department—an area that lies just beyond the library's general fiction shelves, out in the open. Most of the acts were from the Cincinnati area at first, but by the time the fall rolled around their roster had expanded to include acts from Dayton . . . and then Brooklyn! The performances often included new work or collaborations as well as projected images, and they were *weird*. And yet, performances in the series averaged about 40 attendees, with a whopping 156 people turning out for a special screening of Murnau's 1922 silent film *Nosferatu* (figure 5.1). Steve invited a group of six experimental/noise musicians to play a live soundtrack for the film, and the audience was treated to a performance that included traditional instruments like the clarinet, cello, and percussion alongside electronic instruments like the theremin and circuit-bent devices like a modified toy karaoke machine and a contact microphone submerged in dry ice. One of the musicians, a veteran of the experimental music scene, said it was the best-attended performance he'd ever been to.

The Experimental Music at the Library series is a quality example of the Creative Library in action, not because it was successful (the playful, curious nature of the Creative Library means that many things you throw at the wall won't stick, but you'll learn a lot), but because it balances many needs, finds new and exciting ways to meet them, and transforms one person's passionate interest into knowledge and experience for a whole community.

We want to be clear: this isn't an accident. Steve was deliberate about how he contextualized his interest when he set about building a library program. He describes his goals this way:

> The basic idea behind this series is to make the library a space for innovation and incubation . . . a place where musicians can try out new things, exchange ideas, and make connections between their creative output and our extensive collection of recordings. Another goal is to expand library customers' horizons via exposure to new or unfamiliar sonic possibilities.

Experimental Music at the Library was a pet project, but it was a pet project with clear goals that served a broader educational and recreational mission, as well as a community-building one. Steve's program responded to his library's core values and mission by connecting people with new information—information they weren't likely to find in the usual ways, given the niche nature of experimental music. He arranged for people to meet and connect, thereby creating a space and a venue for a particular artist community while also creating a learning opportunity for curious listeners. And he connected all of it back to the library by inviting music acts to share their influences and then exhibiting the library's collection in displays that patrons could browse for more music and more info.

Fig. 5.1 Poster Featuring Film Screening with Live Experimental Soundtrack

Here's how one patron—an older adult—summed up her experience of an early show, where an artist played a loud microtonal sound collage using modified and homemade electronic instruments, including a radio tuned to static playing through an old furnace air filter: "Was that even music? What do you call that? I don't dislike it . . . I just have no idea what to call it. I actually really enjoy it, but it's like nothing else I've ever heard!" For Steve, this commentary meant that his enthusiastic experiment was on the right track: someone in the audience had discovered an entirely new genre of music that she never knew existed.

It's clear that Steve's interest in and experience with experimental music is the crux here, something that informed his program but also gave him the momentum to build a broader community where only an insular one had existed before. Here's what he had to say to other librarians who might want to try out an experimental music program:

> I would say the first step is to seek out and start attending experimental shows in your area. My experience has been, no matter what the city, the community will be small and tightly knit. If you like what you hear and think it might be suitable for your library, strike up a conversation with the musician(s). If you aren't sure where to find experimental music:
>
> - Check your city's weekly alternative paper for music happening in galleries, particularly in artist-run spaces.
> - If you have a college or art school in your city, look for bars and coffee shops where the art kids hang out.
> - Look for photocopied show posters with words like "drone," "ambient," and "noise." If a show is held in someone's living room, a U-Haul truck, or an abandoned building, you're probably on the right track.

BOOKLESS AT THE MADISON PUBLIC LIBRARY

> A big empty space, artists, musicians, drinks, librarians . . . what more could you want?
>
> —*Trent Miller*

At the end of 2011, the Madison Public Library closed the Central Library in downtown Madison, Wisconsin. The building was a 1960s behemoth that hadn't been updated in decades. The children's area was on the second floor, was far too small, and was leaking; the computers were crammed into the reference section; the stacks were too tight despite constant weeding; there was no teen section to speak of; and the cramped quarters of the main library were built for collections and activities long past, while the lower stacks were unusable as anything but an archive, cut off from the rest of the library in the basement (shown in figure 5.2).

The Central Library was still well-loved and well-used, but a new design—something light and modern and *functional*—was in order. So the building was closed, staff members were temporarily reassigned to other branches, and projects were put on hold. The building was emptied of furniture, and miles and miles of stacks were dismantled and packed away into storage. And then the building was empty, waiting for demolition and rebuilding slated for 2012.

And in that empty, bookless library, Trent Miller had a *really* good idea.

Trent is a painter by training; at the time, he worked as a library assistant and served as the gallery coordinator for the Madison

Fig. 5.2 Central Library basement before BOOKLESS, 2013

Public Library, meshing his work life and his creative life as best he could by making connections, inviting local artists to show work and coordinating shows, and promoting the library as a place to get creative work in front of people who might never see it otherwise. So where everyone else saw an empty building and a looming traffic problem with construction, Trent saw an opportunity: why not fill the empty space with art and music and throw a huge party—giving the community one last chance to say goodbye to the library that most of them had known all their lives?

He pitched his idea for a one-day event that would also be a fund-raiser, and BOOKLESS got the green light. Trent put out a call to artists, and received a huge response. "When you say big, open, empty industrial space to most artists, their eyes start to light up," he said. "Some artists brought in older work, but a lot of artists made new work specifically for the space." In the end, Trent worked with 100 artists who contributed a range of artwork and installations, from large-scale paintings and sculpture to photography and video installations.

Trent worked with other staff at MPL and the Madison Public Library Foundation to organize the events of BOOKLESS, including a daytime session for children and families, and a nighttime event called "Party in the Stacks." On January 28, 2012, the building was plastered with art, ranging from works hanging on the walls and ceilings to room-sized installations. Community members created their own art on the huge public painting wall and stations run by local arts organizations. Men in white jumpsuits wandered the floor, creating on-the-spot hot pink BOOKLESS screen prints. Bands played where the old fiction section used to stand, while a dance party thumped along with DJs and video installations in the basement's lower stacks, aptly renamed "Bibliotheque Discotheque." Members of Madison's art community happily caught up with friends and made new ones at the huge party. Hundreds (and hundreds) of community members waited in a line that wrapped around the block in the January cold to get inside and then spent the evening roaming the library, taking it all in. In a single day, the MPL Foundation made over $30,000 from the event, but more importantly, the community got to say goodbye to their library and anticipate a new era, where the library wasn't just about books, but would also be a venue for artistic expression.

"It was a way to look back and celebrate the old building," Trent says, "but it was also a way to look to the future of what we could expect with a new, exciting, dynamic space. Libraries are changing, and we wanted this event to help spotlight the fact that we're excited for the future of ours."

BOOKLESS was so successful that it helped launched Trent into a new role in the MPL as head of The Bubbler, the makerspace and service suite that focuses on bringing creative learning opportunities to every neighborhood in Madison by connecting practicing artists with interested patrons, hosting an artist residency, and empowering patrons to use the library in unexpected and creative ways. We profile The Bubbler in depth in chapter 8, "The Creative Library Platform in Practice," but the important thing to know is that it all started with the passion of one staff member who, with the help and support of some committed colleagues, was given permission to bring his creative talent into the library—the *empty* library— and fill it with something new and exciting that ignited the imagination of the whole community.

RABBLE AND MUSICAT

This is a story about treating fellowship or practicum placements at your library like staff—with trust and professionalism—and the big dividends this kind of support can pay. In this case, the benefit didn't fall to one library, but to librarianship as a whole.

In 2014, Kelly Hiser was completing her PhD in music history at the University of Wisconsin–Madison. She was one of a handful of students who won a Public Humanities Fellowship, a program that works to create professional opportunities outside of academia for humanities graduate students. The goal is to place fellows where their skills can have real-world impact in local organizations and institutions by working on a project at a high level and collaborating with professionals. Kelly's fellowship took place at Madison Public Library (MPL), and her work during her time there focused on a question many libraries grapple with as content creation—not just consumption—becomes *de rigueur* in the library space: how do we share all the stuff the people in our community make? How do we make our collective creative work accessible in the same way we make sure everyone can lay hands on the latest best seller?

This question was especially pressing at MPL because The Bubbler—the burgeoning arts and making platform—focused on creative, hands-on learning opportunities as a library service. Patrons across the city were creating a lot of exciting new content every week in classes and workshops led by local artists, and at events and skillshares in and outside of the library building. The Bubbler's invitations were helping people explore their creativity, and what they made was essentially a document of life in the city, rendered in a collage of stop-motion animations, poems and stories, videos and recorded music, screen prints, trash sculptures, and more.

Kelly focused on the conundrum of hosting and sharing digital art created in the library, since that was the thornier problem: first, because this was where The Bubbler and MPL's teen services intersected, meaning that many content creators were under age; and second, because exponentially more people are able to view an artwork posted online than might ever walk past it in a brick-and-mortar location, and volume raises the stakes. She talked to dozens of librarians across the country to see whether and how they were getting permission to share their patrons' digital content. She found what you might expect: there isn't one right answer, only solutions that work best for individual libraries, their goals, and their communities. Some chose not to share work at all. Some had blanket licenses similar to the signs some libraries post during invitations to alert patrons to the practice of photographing or recording the sessions they produce. Some created official forms and procedures for doing so.

However—one thing Kelly learned through these conversations is a crucial point in the broader shift to the Creative Library that we advocate here: the relationship between patron and library changes when there is a license involved. Kelly summed it up for us in a post on the Library as Incubator Project website in September 2014:

> There are compelling reasons other than legal ones for creating a license in this situation. First, a license provides clarity about the library's intentions

to patrons who might have concerns about the visibility of their or their child's work online. Perhaps even more importantly, though, a license signals a new kind of relationship between a library and a patron, in which the library acts as a platform and publisher by sharing a work more broadly than its creator could do on her own. And whether the library is doing that for a teen's first digital art project or for an established performer's new music video, that's pretty exciting.

At the same time, Kelly and a team of library staff were using her expertise on licensing and sharing locally created content to work with software developers from Murfie, a company that specialized in streaming and downloadable digital music collections, to build a digital catalog prototype for sharing local music. The goal was to create a platform that would not only respond to the library's needs (catalog integration, records, and searchability—all of which are very different than those of a commercial service), but also deliver a streamlined and intuitive browsing experience for patrons.

What they built became the backbone of the groundbreaking MUSICat catalog, and a spinoff startup company called Rabble, where Kelly Hiser is now chief operating officer working alongside the original Murfie team. Each page in a MUSICat library's website not only integrates with the library's catalog, but also functions as a landing page—patrons can download the band's album, and they can also browse through photos, a biography, and links to the band's social media and websites for more information. This model not only connects library patrons with new music through their local library for free, it also helps local acts get the word out with some free online marketing, all of which is delivered in a clean website that looks and feels professional, is easy to navigate, and integrates with the larger system catalog.

We asked Kelly to share the progress Rabble and MUSICat have made since her fellowship at MPL, when the nascent platform was born:

An Update on Rabble and MUSICat

Four years ago, Rabble started working with public libraries to build an open source tool that could capture, share, and amplify the creative efforts of local music communities. The result is MUSICat, an ever-evolving platform that empowers libraries to collect, curate, license, and publish local music online. We now work with over a dozen libraries, including our newest partners in Portland, Pittsburgh, Salt Lake City, and Austin.

Last fall, Rabble launched MUSICat Chorus, a version of the platform for libraries serving smaller populations. Libraries and musicians exist in communities of all sizes, and we're excited to help them imagine new ways to contribute to the public good together.

Over the past year, we've added functionality to MUSICat that helps libraries connect with their communities in new ways. Librarians are inviting local music leaders to curate playlists and are partnering with local nonprofits to showcase historical material in MUSICat. We are also streamlining how we support librarians using MUSICat. That meant documenting best practices we've learned with our library partners; crafting a more deliberate consulting process to support project managers as they develop promotion, policy, and community engagement; and managing an ongoing conversation among a group of librarians who are building local music collections.

Perhaps the most exciting part of our work is seeing how "creative libraries" like MUSICat sites are more than repositories for digital content, but are part of vibrant creative feedback loops. The libraries we work with aren't just publishing music: they're collaborating with their communities to curate collections; they're providing instruments, tools, and education for musicians; and they're hosting shows with local venues. In short, they're continuously engaging their creative communities by building collections and programming together. Our task is to help librarians figure out how technology can amplify those collaborative efforts in ways that build public good for communities.

—*Kelly Hiser*

....

This is one of our favorite Creative Library platform stories because it is (unusually!) seamless: a collaborative fellowship placement from a local university who plays a key role in the project; a local business that contributes its tech expertise to the project; a product that creates access to and community around local music; and an exciting spin-off company that can bring the whole idea to more libraries, documenting more local collections and bringing more music to more people.

WHAT DO THESE EXAMPLES HAVE IN COMMON?

- They create community
- They create connections with partners
- They showcase an expansive approach to the mission of the library
- They are examples of the growth mindset at work

The growth mindset is a crucial part of these successes. Each person's project began as an exploration or experiment—one that could have failed but was given some low-stakes room to try and see what would happen. Other experiments fail brilliantly and produce usable information about *why* a certain kind of program doesn't work, providing a useful checklist for future attempts. Because the library is a space for lifelong learning, it makes sense to extend this concept *inward*, to the learning process that takes place when staff commit to experimenting with their work in order to find the best methods and innovations possible—an ongoing process.

GETTING STARTED

The Creative Library requires a light touch, and a certain element of play and curiosity. This can be a challenge to nurture in a profession where workers have more to do than time to do it in, and often have to do it in spaces that are inadequate. But that's the beauty of creativity—if you create the right climate for it, even in the most cursory way, it blossoms. Your staff comes ready-made with hidden talents, community ties, and passion projects, but they need to know that their workplace is a safe space to show off a bit, to dream big and explore possibilities. Once they do, *all sorts* of ideas will bubble to the surface, and it's worth thinking through how to give those ideas some space and room to become a *thing*. Not all of them will, of course, but the point isn't to bring every single idea to fruition. It's to continuously learn and experiment with what's possible

Here, we want to focus on three clear opportunities for connection and playful shake-ups of the normal routine that can help staff begin to feel more supported as creative contributors. We include two exercises at the end of this chapter that can be great tools for breaking the ice with your staff and doing a reset to tee up your creative library goals.

Onboarding (or Re-Onboarding)

Often, the person you know least about on your staff is quietly doing something extraordinary on her own time: connecting with a different subset of the community, brewing her own *kombucha* tea in a scary basement, or designing the perfect slingshot.

Knowing your staff is vital.

No, we're not talking about knowing whether one person needs a false deadline to make sure she hits the real deadline; we're talking about knowing that one of your part-time evening staffers went to school for film and still blogs about it. You have to know your staffers as people—to care about their lives, their creative practice, their interests. What makes you think: "Hmmm. How did you end up here?" Someone on your library's staff probably studied film for a while. Another staffer might be a triathlete or the bassist in a hard-core metal band. Some people wear their interests on their sleeve and share their lives readily, but others need a little prodding—and some genuine interest shown in them—to understand that their workplace is a safe space to showcase their hobbies and passions.

The welcome (and good manners and genuine interest) that we extend to potential patrons should also extend to the folks we work with. Yes, even the staffer who brushes her cat and makes felted toys out of its fur. Come on! She knows how to make felted toys!

You should consider onboarding as an opportunity to ask nondirected questions the way you might canvass your community asking "What would make our town better?" and then thinking up ways the library could help with the answers. Why not ask your staff a few oddball questions aimed at getting a read on their internal weather? Here are a few:

- What would be your ideal job?
- What are your secret talents?
- What did you think was the coolest job when you were a kid?
- If you could add one feature to the library, what would it be?

The point isn't to ask "What kinds of invitations do you want to work on?" and then dump your staff into those buckets. The point is to learn some interesting facts about a *person*. Facts might eventually coalesce into an opportunity: if someone says "I always thought working in the paint department at Home Depot would be awesome when I was a kid. I love color," or "My ideal job would be interior design—I love to make beautiful spaces," that might eventually be the person you recruit to design and install gallery shows in the library.

If you're rebooting your library as a creative library, we think a little re-on-boarding is a good place to start. Try out the two exercises we include at the end of this chapter for ideas, or invent a survey—with prizes!—for everyone to share.

Involving Staff across Departments

In all of the examples we have shared in this chapter, big and small, multiple people on staff had some stake in the project, from concept, to build, to understanding it and sharing it with patrons. We found that the organizations with the most success approached invitations like these, and the platforms they were part of, with the assumption that they were vital library services, not some flash-in-the-pan extra. No one was saying, *oh, that will go by the wayside, don't bother to learn it, just wait it out.* Programming isn't some cute add-on that has nothing to do with the real library (we're pretty sure if you're reading this, we don't have to tell you that). Staff participation and knowledge of these invitations were enthusiastic and competent across departments and specialties.

We think this is an important point: the creative library, particularly invitations, are a core competency for staff. Everyone who goes for a job in a library understands that they will be involved in the life cycle of library books in some way. Maybe they will purchase them, or catalog and process them. Perhaps they will look them up for patrons, perform story times with them, move giant bins of them from library to library, or arrange them on shelves. Maybe they will check them in and out. But we often hear that some folks who work in libraries don't think they are involved in invitations. When those come up, they panic; someone who can look up even the most obscure title ("I think the cover was green?") and find it on the shelf for a patron balks at finding the same kind of information about invitations and the resources associated with them. You'd have to have a long, frank chat with someone on your staff if she never told a patron where they could find the kids' nonfiction and instead directed patrons to the selector of that collection. So why is this acceptable behavior when it comes to the invitations on your programming calendar?

The fundamental problem is one of perspective—the folks who think libraries are about *books* tend to feel suddenly incapable when they are expected to field questions about events and invitations. But the folks who think libraries are about *information* and *learning* realize that an invitation can deliver just as much valuable information as a book on the same topic—and sometimes even more.

Here are a few simple ways to work toward a staff that feels confident with all the pieces of the Creative Library platform:

- Shift your language. Talk with people from every department about how their work fits into the larger goal of surfacing information in different forms—books, experiences, exhibits, and so on—so that patrons can use this information to learn what they want to learn in the best mode for them. This means hosting cooking workshops and collecting cookbooks, and for both selectors and programming librarians to be able to see their work as fundamentally the same.
- Talk about invitations the way you talk about collections. We'll touch on this more in chapter 7, "The Lenses: Evaluation," but it's worth bringing up here: your programming calendar is part of your collection. So your basic expectation of your staff would be that everyone is able to direct people to invitations with the same facility they can direct them to the fiction section when asked. Talking about invitations as a collection helps to mitigate some of the anxiety some library folks can have about new or unfamiliar expectations. They already know all about collection stuff.
- Understand that invitations turn over fast—so arm staff with the information they need. Some of the anxiety that library people feel comes from the dynamic nature of events and programs. The fiction section is always there, but the invitations on your calendar change every week. Make sure that your staff know how to search and filter your library's online events calendar with the same confidence they bring to the catalog they've been working with for years, so that when a patron asks about the Farmer's Market Cooking series, they will be able to find the event listing and communicate its time and date, what the basic gist of the program is, whether sign-ups are necessary, and so on. And just as you may already have collection updates for all staff about high-demand holds or new releases, consider providing regular updates on programs of note, with brief talking points for front-line staff about early sign-ups, when registrations go live, and any related resources that are part of the same platform.

Annual Planning Retreat

Another space where the creative library can get the best from its staff is in annual planning retreats. Some of you are already rolling your eyes—as if there's any time to take away from the checking-in and repairing, and answering users' questions! We believe you; we've been there. But please consider taking the time to really assess a year in the life of the library, with input on initiatives, support, crazy times when one more thing just isn't feasible, and opportunities to draw in more people; in other words, by gathering input from all members of the staff. This is a golden opportunity. They're your front-line crew, after all. Shouldn't they have a say in what the library does over the course of the year?

One excellent example comes to us from Janie Hermann at the Princeton (NJ) Public Library, who annually hosts a retreat for the programming team— these are a motley crew of library staff at all levels who are *interested in programming*. Janie's programming team doesn't include just "staff" per se—she's got a passionate and excited lineup of people from throughout her library. Her crew includes librarians and assistants, circulation staff, pages, and volunteers. All of them are interested in library events—or a particular event—and are eager and excited to spend some of their working hours helping out in an area they are passionate about.

Janie is a powerhouse of invitation know-how, but the Princeton Library's calendar isn't her brainchild; she doesn't come up with that stuff all on her own. She relies on the interests of her team to guide her—sometimes into places she wouldn't have dreamed of going.

Every August, the programming staff get together for a half-day retreat (with lunch) and look at two things:

- They assess last year's programs, and consider whether any of them should be weeded out of the calendar (more on this in chapter 7, "The Lenses: Evaluation").
- They look at the next year and consider what they want to do.

Planning the programs for the next year involves every department's expertise, and every person's knowledge—everything is considered, from community events and anniversaries (Einstein's 100th birthday, events happening on Princeton University's campus, local festivals, farmer's markets, celebrations) to ALA-sponsored events (Library Card Sign-up Month, Teen Tech Week), to author book tours, collection trends that indicate opportunities for programs, and special events (like the Children's Book Expo and the Environmental Film Festival). Everyone on the team shares program ideas—ideas for how the library can be involved in the town, how it can respond to stated and implied community needs and grant-related programs, and their own interests or dream programs they would love to do. *Everyone.* Janie writes down every idea. Some get put on the docket right away, and some of them—especially pie-in-the-sky wish list programs—don't come together right away. But they stay on the list, and some of them bubble away on the back burner until the right opportunity presents itself.

These people *care* about the programs they work on. They love this part of their job, and their input and enthusiasm drive some exciting projects.

RECOMMENDED EXERCISES

Here are a couple of exercises we love that can be used during onboarding with new staff, re-onboarding existing staff (especially if you're looking to do a creative library reboot), or at in-service days, retreats, or team meetings. The goal is to break the ice, lighten the mood, and generate a playful new perspective on how the library works and what it is for. Remember, the core of what we do is connecting people with information. This transaction is often pretty straightforward: you point the patron to the murder mysteries or the *Consumer Reports* database, or you recommend a new title or a local group that can help. But sometimes this transaction is more about *revealing* information. What makes a person laugh? What makes them curious? What inspires them? This happens less often, but you'll know the libraries where it doesn't happen *at all*—they're the ones that seem dead inside, full of information, and none of it sparking anything new.

Exploring this part of the connecting-people-with-information exchange—the part that is less well-defined, and is full of possibility—is what we hope you'll try with your staff.

.... *ele* ....

Invitations for Librarians

- STACK PIECE 1
  Take a row of books and imagine how they could be arranged differently. Then do it.

- STACK PIECE 2
  Record the number of laughs heard in the stacks:
  1. In the morning
  2. In the afternoon
  3. In the evening

  If no one is laughing in the stacks, install something, and try again tomorrow.

- SHUSHING PIECE
  Instead of shushing, encourage everyone in the library to speak louder.
  Encourage those already speaking loudly to sing.
  Invite those already singing to dance.

- CITY PIECE 1
  Create mini-libraries of five books or less in bus stations around town.

- RESEARCH PIECE
  Envision a research guide that a houseplant might want to use. Create it.

- REFERENCE DESK PIECE
  Disband the reference desk for the day.
  Invite patrons to sit at tables and allow other patrons to ask them their questions (figure 5.3).

Fig. 5.3
Invitations for Librarians

- DICTIONARY PIECE 1
  Get a large scroll of paper.
  Instead of looking up a word in the dictionary, patrons write the word that they want defined.
  Patrons who know a word on the scroll write what it means to them.
  Catalog the scroll for reference. Keep it full of paper.

- DICTIONARY PIECE 2
  Take old dictionaries and let the children draw in them. Distribute the drawings to people in the library.

- CATALOGER'S PIECE
  Write a short poem and hide it in each book you catalog today.

- CITY PIECE 2
  Wear a sign that says "I'm a librarian" all day. Help people where they are.

—Lauren Gottlieb-Miller, illustrated by Oliver Bendorf;
inspired by Yoko Ono's book, Grapefruit.[3]

Give and Take

WHAT DO YOU KNOW? WHAT DO YOU WANT TO KNOW? Knowledge and curiosity are the catalysts for Give & Take, a public art project created by Works Progress in 2009. We launched Give & Take as a series of monthly gatherings at Intermedia Arts in Minneapolis to encourage relationships, reciprocity, and resilience in our community. Initial funding came from a Metropolitan Regional Arts Council Community Arts Grant. The project has since evolved into an open-source public engagement project that opens space for the face-to-face exchange of ideas and resources in many different communities.[4]

The setup for this creativity-friendly exercise is so simple that it's hard to justify not trying it out: each person in a group (a community partners meet-up, a staff day, a team retreat) wears a nametag (figure 5.4) that includes not just their preferred name and pronouns but also two other pieces of information:

- What they know
- What they want to know

The goal of this introductory/ice-breaker activity is to connect with people who know what you want to learn about, and strike up conversations. It sounds simple, right? It might even sound kind of hokey. But the results are inspiring—not only do most people really enjoy this activity (even anxious, introverted types

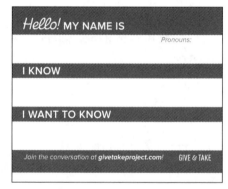

Fig. 5.4 Give & Take Nametag

are put at ease by having clear parameters for the discussion), but it can foster unexpected and unexpectedly exuberant connections. Maybe your cubicle mate, who you've worked next to for months, knows Ruby, and you've been thinking of adding to the programming languages you know. Or say there's a community group in town that just can't seem to follow through on requests to connect, but you've managed to forge a connection with someone in the group because both of you enjoy the nerdy viciousness of speed chess—something you plan to leverage when you reach out again.

These kinds of connections happen all the time during Give and Take, in addition to cross-departmental kismet that brings catalogers and programming librarians together over a shared love of *Doctor Who* or an ambition to hike through the Appalachian Trail. Folks who might as well have been on another planet at the beginning of the meeting suddenly have an interesting, personal connection—a sense of kinship—that not only fosters goodwill and opens up potential collaborations, but also makes it harder to blow someone off. You're connected now—and you wouldn't blow off a fellow Whovian, WOULD YOU?

Consider adding a gentle reminder that these extra bits of personal info should be nonwork-related, or at least not directly related—they should be an interest or passion that isn't in the daily grind of work.

Notes

1. Connect with Jessica at handmadelibrarian.com and @handmadelibrary on Twitter. We also highly recommend her book, *Bibliocraft*.
2. Medium, https://medium.com/@joshuaaromin/the-unicorn-of-things-making-friends -as-an-adult-79f6b24537c9.
3. WorldCat, https://www.worldcat.org/title/grapefruit/oclc/16194397&referer=brief _results.
4. Works Progress, www.worksprogress.org/new-page.

THE LENSES: COMMUNITY-LED INVITATIONS

ONE OF THE AMAZING THINGS THAT WE APPRECIATE ABOUT the library community, across departments and user groups, is that people are willing to share a *lot* of ideas and successes when it comes to library invitations and initiatives. Blogs, Pinterest, Twitter chats, Facebook groups and pages, the idea-sharing and trading, the questions and troubleshooting tips—your colleagues around the world harbor a wealth of best practices and experiences that should not go untapped.

Sometimes you see an idea or an invitation that happened at another library, and you think, *yes*, that's a perfect fit, because my neighborhood is all about cooking workshops, and I'm going to ask my partner at such-and-such organization if they'd like to cohost, and I bet Chef So-and-So will be pumped to facilitate and can recommend other facilitators. At other times, you feel like you're taking ideas that worked super well for communities across the country, or even just one town over, and it's falling flat.

Instead of throwing invitation idea after idea at the wall to see what will stick, we want to encourage you to take a step back and think about reorienting your resources so that your community, the people who use—or don't use—the library, have the opportunity to drive when it comes to invitation or initiative planning. The result may not be what you expected, but that's part of the point—that you're cultivating the right space for people to pitch and run with their own ideas.

There's another, more important reason to reorient your programming to be community-led or community-driven, and that has to do with power.[1] Librar-

<95>

ies, no matter what their size or kind, are institutions. Institutions have power, and usually that power is tied to a historic system that was built and established specifically to keep one group of people in power over another. Libraries of all kinds have historically been "white spaces" because of a variety of policies and practices, and while the library workforce is *slowly* becoming more diverse, white folks still make up a significant majority of librarians and library assistants.[2] Working to give up power by turning over resources to community groups is *part* of a wider process that institutions like libraries must do in order to disman-tle the long-standing white-dominated, patriarchal, ableist structures that have influenced modern library collections and services throughout history.

We are not claiming to be experts on these matters; rather, as white women working in LIS and other information fields (and therefore often unwittingly perpetuating the status quo), we are working to educate ourselves, to listen to colleagues, patrons, and non-patrons—particularly people of color and others in historically underrepresented groups—and to pay attention to movements like Black Lives Matter, #ownvoices, #metoo, and others in order to understand our role as librarians and our work's wider implications in social justice movements. For many, the library *is* a safe and welcoming place, but this is not the case for all community members. Doing what we can to not create wider rifts or do more damage (unintentional though that damage may be) is really important.

MOVING TO YES

One place to start in support of community-led creativity initiatives is to create a culture of "yes" at your library, at all staffing levels and across departments.[3] But even as I typed this, I thought, *oh no*—usually we're trying to figure out how to say *no* to more things in order to free up calendar space and head-space for larger, more meaningful projects. If we say "yes" to everything, that's going to end badly.

Saying "yes" when it comes to community-led initiatives does not mean host-ing every invitation or event idea that comes your way. We get lots of event and program pitches at our libraries—far too many to host well. But many of these come from people who are not in the library's service area, much less the imme-diate neighborhood. For us to want to work with these folks, their pitch really needs to be timely and something that we know our neighborhood will be inter-ested in—because we'd rather be working with our own community on what *they* want to do. It's perfectly okay to say "no" in order to keep space and resources available for people who are working on the local level and want to leverage those resources to expand their work.

Just as we discussed in chapter 3, you can feel free to take a break from an existing invitation series or "reverse-pilot" a time-consuming invitation or service in order to free up space to fully support community-led initiatives.

The examples in this chapter represent a handful of possibilities for ways to create a climate where the community can lead and determine what the library does, and how it handles and distributes resources.

To varying degrees, in these examples:

1. The library plays a supporting role, and is not the sole driver/instigator.
1. How the library distributes its resources is driven by the community.

EXAMPLE: LIBRARY TAKEOVER

Library Takeover is an initiative that originated in the United Kingdom as a collaboration between a performance poetry organization, Apples & Snakes, and Half-Moon Theatre, a theater company.[4] Staff from these two organizations developed a training program for teams of library staff and local students who were 11 to 18 years old; the program would last for twelve weeks and take place after school hours and on weekends at the library. The teams learned the ins and outs of ideating, planning, and hosting "live creative events" in library spaces. The resulting events of the first iteration of Library Takeover were Urban Explosion, a youth-led poetry slam, and a Literary Fashion Show, wherein youth designers created their own fashion apparel out of recycled materials, with a literary bent. Both of these events were designed to be hosted in library spaces, and were available to be booked after their initial delivery by libraries in neighboring London boroughs. Below is Laura's account of a Library Takeover that she coordinated.

Library Takeover at the Madison Public Library

When I took a job as a community engagement librarian for the Central Library in Madison, Wisconsin, my colleague Kylee and I spent the first several months of our new jobs talking with community organizations that were focused on education and learning for adults. Our scope was broader than The Bubbler's, so we had a wider net that eventually included most of the city's neighborhood and community centers, as well as adult education organizations like the Literacy

Network. Our conversations with these folks helped shape most of the invitations and resources that we would eventually coordinate.

One of the things that our talks kept coming back to was that people already have great ideas for events and initiatives, but they don't always have the resources available to make them happen. Madison's an engaged, but nonprofit-heavy city. Funding opportunities are usually limited to organizations (by and large usually staffed by white folks), and grant programs that are accessible to unaffiliated community members are still bound by a lot of rules and paperwork. Might there be an opportunity for the library to turn over some of its resources to community members who otherwise might not have access to funding?

A platform like Library Takeover, which is designed to offer resources paired with training in community event planning, seemed like a way to pilot a community-led event series in a holistic way. After a consultation with the project's British originators, we pitched Library Takeover to the Madison Public Library Foundation in their 2016 grant cycle. Key changes to the platform as we presented it in the grant application included:

- The program would be targeted to adults, rather than high school students.
- The workshop schedule would be pared down from twelve weeks to a six-week boot camp.
- Because of the shortened training time frame, we would ask for teams of community members to pitch specific event ideas (these could be broad) rather than including time for ideation in the training workshops.

The library was awarded $18,000 to move forward with Library Takeover in 2016. The next step for us was to conduct an equity analysis, an interactive tool that the city of Madison utilizes to double-check assumptions and biases that can lead to inequitable policies and, in this case, programs. The tool and process for an equity analysis involve asking a group of people—who are *not* connected to the deployment of the policy or program—to review the policy or program and interrogate it using a set of questions.[5]

Comments during the equity analysis included the following feedback, and led to some key changes in the program structure:

- We need to pay people—the community team members—for their time. Originally the program budget did not include a line item for stipends or honorariums for the team members who would be doing the Library Takeover events. Change: we shifted funds from other pots within the program budget so that we could offer team members an honorarium.

- We need to streamline the application process, or at least take a look at our questions on the application and ask why are we asking this? Change: the application question, "Tell us about any previous event-planning experience that members of the team have," was removed from the application.
- We need to find a way to follow up with teams in case their written application isn't very clear, in order to make sure that they have a chance to explain their idea more fully. Change: we would talk in-person or on the phone with the finalists before making a decision, in order to ask follow-up or clarifying questions.

At the end of it all, this is a snapshot of Library Takeover, Year One:

Big picture:
- Three teams' event ideas were selected for participation.
- Teams get an event budget, free space, free marketing and promotional help, expertise from presenters, library staff, and a team mentor.

Application process:
- Six-week-long window to apply. Had lots of media exposure, social media exposure, word of mouth, and e-mail announcements.
- Teams applied with 3–5 members. Nonprofit organizations, city agencies, or other preexisting groups were not eligible to apply for the program, since the goal was to help unaffiliated community members reach their event goals.
- Applications were accepted online via Google Forms, in hard copy on printouts, and over the phone. The staff at all library locations were given instructions and an FAQ so that they could talk about the program and assist people with filling out the applications.

Program staff:
- The library contracted with six presenters to talk about different topics related to event planning during the six-week-long boot camp.
- Three mentors with previous event-planning experience were hired to be nonlibrary staff points of contact who could bounce around ideas, ask questions, and offer suggestions or advice as needed during the process.
- Two librarians, myself and Kylee, were the leads on program coordination, overseeing the boot camp, and the overall logistics, while two other locations designated a staff contact person at their location to liaise with the teams whose events were selected for their libraries.

- We also had a library school student intern, who documented the entire boot-camp process and team updates to make sure we had content for reporting back to the foundation.
- A lot of additional library staff supported the events in some way, ranging from our maintenance team who did program setup, to our marketing staff who put in hours helping with promotional materials and publicity.

Selection process:

- Kylee and I took an initial pass at the forty (!) idea pitches the library received, and we weeded out any incomplete applications or applications that did not meet the minimum requirements.
- Applications were stripped of names and contact information in order to try to keep it as "blind" a process as possible.
- Ideas were sent to a panel that included presenters and library staff members. These folks used a basic rubric to apply scores to the ideas.
- The top ten scoring ideas were then sent to the three team mentors, who also applied scores to these pitches.
- The top three ideas were presented to members of library administration, who gave the ultimate okay.

Event-planning boot camp:

- Workshops were held on topics that included marketing, finances/budgeting, production or "day-of" considerations, and event or program evaluation.
- Dinner was offered at each workshop.
- Child care was available upon request by the participants.
- The workshops took place primarily in The Bubbler Room at the Central Library.
- The workshops included presentations, Q&A, and work time for teams to talk about their progress with their mentor.

Now, it all seems pretty tidy on paper, right? Teams come in, they learn a thing, and then they apply that thing to their actual event. You probably don't need me to tell you that planning events is *hard*. There are so many working parts to keep track of, especially when the community members involved are working with a team and an institution, even one that is *hopefully* doing its best to say yes whenever possible. As a staff member trying to be a resource for a community group, it can be really hard to sit back and not (a) micromanage the team or (b) stress out big time if there are periods of quiet while the team is working out details on their own. Figuring out your role within the team's planning structure can take a little while, and that role may vary depending on how involved the team prefers you to be.

The events:

ACCESS DENIED—this was part community panel, and part dance party. The topic to explore was: what makes for a truly accessible, welcoming nightlife space and experience, in particular for marginalized communities? A group of community members made up the panel and tackled big questions about barriers to nightlife and what venue owners, staff, and other partygoers can do to help create a welcoming space for undocumented folks, people of color, women, people who are sober, people who are LGBTQ, and folks with varying abilities, mobilities, and neurodiversity. *Team members: Sarah Akawa, Jean Brody, King Shabazz, Ti Banks, Alix Shabazz.*

SHARE THE WORD—this was a networking, social, and performance event for writers of different kinds, backgrounds, and experiences in the Madison area. Writers of all stripes came together to hear presentations of local authors' works, and to have connecting conversations about their work and opportunities for collaboration. A local band played, a local restaurant catered, and a diverse cross-section of Madison's writing community offered readings of poetry and hip-hop. *Team members: Oscar Mireles, Zora Beach, Diana Gonzales, Joey Phelps.*

NAMASTE MADISON—this was an event and exhibition designed to amplify and celebrate the many contributions of Madison's diverse Indian and Indian American community to Madison and the surrounding area since the first international students from India began to study at the University of Wisconsin in the 1960s. The team used their event budget to produce a set of twenty high-quality posters and banners that were displayed throughout the Central Library for a week leading up to a daylong event with community panels, food demonstrations, and children's activities. *Team members: Lakshmi Sridharan, Anjali Sridharan, Pratibha Antani, Neeta Saluja, Amitha Domalpally.*

Overall, our first time out with Library Takeover was a success. Three events happened, lots of people came, first-round participants learned a lot (and so did the library), and the teams had solid feedback that we could use to make edits to the next round of Takeover.

The second round of Library Takeover, started with the boot camp in the spring of 2018 and wrapped up in May of 2019 with the last of three events. These events were, LOVE, INSHALLAH, an evening of love stories told through a Muslim lens; NOURISH YOU, a self-care retreat produced by women for women who may not feel comfortable or welcome in mainstream wellness spaces; and most recently, MANY VOICES, ONE COMMUNITY BLOCK PARTY, a celebration and amplification of the low-power community radio station WWMV-LP 95.5.

This is not to say that there were no hiccups, obstacles, and challenges that we encountered during the first and second rounds of Library Takeover. Coordinating the platform is a *lot* of work, and it requires a *lot* of resources, both financial and, most importantly and draining, time resources for both staff and the community teams. Even though this platform is built with the goal of amplifying historically underrepresented groups and ideas, there are still a lot of moments when that goal runs up against institutional policies, practices, and bureaucratic hoops that uphold a white-dominated system. Things like preferred vendor lists and no-selling policies, even where the library is located, can be barriers to access; if not for the teams, then for the people they want to come to their event. This was a really good reminder for me that even though the whole platform feels like the library is doing exactly that—giving up power—that power is not only about turning over resources to community groups. It's built into our systems and the structures that inform all of our policies and practices. Library Takeover could knock down some barriers to access, but it is not a be-all end-all solution.

Takeover Takeaways

We learned so many lessons from working on this platform for the last two and a half years!

1. People have amazing ideas, and they're usually not at all what you would plan yourself, and that's great.
2. In retrospect, doing the equity analysis before applying for grant funding would have helped ensure that we got on the right track much faster and more efficiently, especially with regard to how we were distributing the funds that we applied for.
3. Don't micromanage. Be available as a resource however you can; send reminders about important deadlines especially if they impact other library departments like marketing or facilities. Be flexible with how you receive and share information; if a team prefers to ask questions by text or using Facebook, is there a way you can meet them where they are?
4. This platform requires a lot of work on the part of library staff, but also on the part of the community teams. Honor that work in any way that you can, whether that is financially, or with a certificate of completion, or a letter of recommendation, or all of these—anything you can do, do.

I am listed as a reference on multiple former team members' resumes, I have written letters of recommendation, and I will happily continue to do so.

5. Everyone is bringing expertise and experience to the table; the library's role should be to listen and amplify the ideas that are already there, *not* assume that "our" way of doing things is the best way.

Through Library Takeover, we hoped to create an interactive way for folks from the community to utilize library resources to deliver large-scale public events. Though it was by no means smooth sailing all the time, Library Takeover did meet this goal, and along the way it provided some really vital insight and feedback to the library about the real-life impact of policies and practices that had previously been taken for granted.[6]

EXAMPLE: ARTISTS IN RESIDENCE

You can think of artist in residence (AIR) initiatives as community-led invitations on a micro-scale, since usually you're only working with one individual or perhaps a very small group of people at one time. AIR initiatives take many forms, depending on the library. Some AIRs are only "in residence" for a very short time, while others may last longer—several weeks or months. AIRs vary widely in what they do in and with the library. Some may emphasize public programming, while others may focus on their own work with the goal of spending time on a particular project that may integrate library resources and research, and still others may simply utilize library space as a studio or demonstration space.

The example AIRs in this section are meant to provide a taste of the different styles of AIR initiatives. It is by no means an exhaustive list. You should follow the Library ArtsLink (shout-out to instigator Trent Miller) on Facebook and on their website to find additional AIR initiatives and to connect directly with staff who can answer questions and provide documentation.

Shaler North Hills Library

Located in Glenshaw, Pennsylvania, the Shaler North Hills Library was home for several years to a vibrant arts initiative known as Art and Inspiration, which was curated by the artist William Rock in partnership with the library.[7] Art and Inspiration had a number of elements (it was basically a creativity platform of its own), ranging from artist dialogues to art classes and a podcast. One artist in particular inspired William Rock to work with the library to establish a one-time artist residency that would be part of the Art and Inspiration platform. Jennifer Meridian (formerly Nagle Myers) wears many hats as an art educator and art collection manager, and of course as a working artist. Her artistic practice "involves storytelling, object-making, and performances that are designed to help me imagine a different and more radical world, one that puts all people and all living systems first. This includes tribute, reenactment, and performance as ways to create the space for this type of imagining."

William Rock spotted the potential for Jenn to connect closely with the community through an artist residency, and so he collaborated with the adult services librarian, Marie Jackson, to establish a unique AIR program that utilized Jenn's skills and also fit the needs of the Shaler North Hills Library community. Marie's response to our question, "What sort of preparations did the library have to do in order to make the residency happen?" goes a long way toward demonstrating what a little intentionality can do when it comes to getting buy-in from the rest of the library to establish a new program with community partners:

> The most important aspect of an Artist in Residence in the library for me was staff awareness of the idea and concept. Our staff is welcoming and attentive to library customers and enthusiastically encourages library users to participate in the programs and events that we offer. I wanted all the staff members to recognize Jennifer when she arrived at the library and to know her role as Artist in Residence. To accomplish this, I invited Jennifer Nagle Myers and William Rock as presenting guests at the library's annual day-long in-service staff meeting which was scheduled one week before Jennifer started her residency. Jennifer was a wonderful guest at our meeting and she charmed the staff with her experiences about self-publishing a book of stories written by her father. She was so engaging that two staff members approached her with their ideas about how she could help them with their creative projects. (They both made appointments with Jennifer during her residency at the library.)

And then Jenn responded to our question: "Jennifer, what was compelling to you about an artist residency in a library? Can you tell us some of your plans for the artist residency?" She positioned herself as almost adding to the library's resources in the form of, well, *herself*:

It is interesting to think about how the artist can be active in her community. There are many ways. Being an artist can be extremely isolating if you let it be. Time spent in the studio can be all-consuming. I realized several years ago that I needed another outlet other than just the studio work/world, and that led me to create performances for site-specific public spaces throughout the city as a way to connect to the world and the people. I am still exploring what that means. Being an artist at a library is one way that this is being explored, as I like to think of the library as a site. I am doing a site-specific residency at this particular wonderful library, that is full of the most supportive and interesting people, and it has been a wonderful and rich experience.

Through dialogue with Bill and Marie, we came up with the idea that this would be an inherently very public residency. The core of the residency is that I am available to be "checked out" during my weekly "office hours," from 1:00–5:00 every Thursday afternoon. So people sign up to "check me out" and schedule 30-minute or one-hour appointments with me, where I provide creative consulting and creative mentoring to anything that they are seeking help with. This can range from patrons needing more information about self-publishing, which I am experienced with, or ideas for how to create a giant collage in their living room with their children. I have met with an eight-year-old who wants to make his own books and a 75-year-old who wants to have a website to share her amazing paintings with the world. Many of the consultations become personal stories and are interesting and compelling ways to experience people in a very intimate and immediate way.

The library serves as a host for an initiative that really is community partner-driven and instigated, and the resources that the community can tap into are deepened through the check-out-an-artist opportunity. Jenn's expertise, her intimate personal knowledge of creative practice, is made accessible to people who may find that conversation and dialogue are the most effective ways for them to work through their questions and creative challenges.[8]

Not every library will be able to fund an artist residency initiative year-round, or even more than once a year. Especially if you're in a small library in a small community, feel free to take this short-term idea and run with it. Maybe there's a check-out-an-artist program every October in preparation for National Novel Writing Month, or in February when people feel like they're in a wintry rut.

Edmonton Public Library Writer in Residence

The writer in residence (WIR) program at Canada's Edmonton Public Library is a collaborative project involving a number of public libraries and library systems in and around Edmonton.[9] The WIR initiative emphasizes utilizing the writers in residence as community resources, by attending workshops and craft talks and by having the writers be available by e-mail, phone, and by appointment for in-person conversations.

WIRs contract with the library and its partners for a year. They are expected to spend 50 percent of their time working on their personal writing projects, and the other 50 percent engaged in public programming and engagement. WIRs are paid approximately $40,000 as independent contractors during their year-long residency, with some additional funding available for public programming. This is an example of a very well-funded, well-supported writer in residence program model, a model that a stand-alone public library or academic library may be unlikely to fund on its own. But with strategic partnerships and collaboration between regional libraries or library systems, it's possible.

Carnegie Library of Pittsburgh-Hazelwood Branch

Information about this residency came to the Library as Incubator Project back in 2015, when Edith Abeyta wrote a series of posts documenting her yearlong artist residency at the Hazelwood branch of the Carnegie Library of Pittsburgh.[10] We highly recommend checking out all four posts in Edith's series, but we want to highlight one particular aspect of this residency, which was to work with neighborhood residents to determine what public art in the neighborhood should entail, encompass, and include:

> It's not unusual for artists to work in the public sphere, but it is not so common for artists to connect with residents in a neighborhood and for the latter to determine the public art. The artist in residency program at CLP-Hazelwood has this as its focus. Initiated by the Office of Public Art, their Artist in the Public Sphere program places artists in neighborhoods to engage with residents to formulate and define the art they want to experience. It is a process that involves connecting with people in a meaningful way. The end result is unknown for everyone who participates.
>
> For six months, I spent time in the library and other locations throughout Hazelwood building relationships with youth, adults, elders, community leaders, activists, advocates, and organizations. At times this manifested as art activities with youth and adults in the library, and most

recently it took the form of meetings to present, discuss, and rank public art projects proposed by residents.

There's nothing mysterious about this process, but it is significant. Hazelwood residents who are engaged and connected to their neighborhood spend a great deal of time at meetings to make sure their voices are heard and their visions are implemented. Many of the people who participated in the public art meetings have been going to countless meetings for years. The subjects of these range from resisting the rebuilding of the LTV Steel's Coke Works in the late 1990s, resisting the proposed closure of the library in the 2000s, and three years of meetings regarding the ALMONO development, in addition to the ones they attend for neighborhood organizations. So to ask these folks to participate in more meetings is a big deal.

We hosted three meetings at the library, the first at the end of January to present the seventeen proposed projects we received. Various community members shared their art ideas in the days and months leading up to this meeting. Most were attainable, so we spent time discussing each idea and viewing images of similar art projects in and outside of Pittsburgh. At the end of the meeting, participants placed dots on the proposals they most wanted to see manifest. From this we narrowed down the proposals to six.

The second meeting was held at the end of February. The focus was a more in-depth examination and brainstorming session on how, why, and where the proposed projects would play out. Locations, longevity, and materials were discussed, as well as expanded explanations of the projects by the residents who proposed them. There was general agreement by participants that they wanted to have ongoing projects/programs with variety throughout the neighborhood and to connect with as many residents as possible.

The third meeting on March 28 was a brief overview and review of the six projects: Second Avenue Portraits, Arts & Culture Excursions, Garden Signs, Gateway Signs, Non-Violent Conflict Resolution Art program, and a fence project. We viewed maps, talked about neighborhood borders, and ranked the projects from 0 to 5. The Arts & Culture Excursion program ranked highest, receiving 93 points. The resident who proposed it envisioned it as a program similar to the Art Research Days we had hosted in November 2014. Future meetings will be scheduled to develop and implement the program but for now, everyone has one less meeting to attend.

This residency and its focus on community visioning utilized the library as an accessible and welcoming neighborhood space for discussion and brainstorming, and as a sort of nexus for coming together to talk about art and how the residents want to experience art in the places where they live. The open-ended nature of Edith's approach meant that ideas could come from anyone and everyone who wanted to participate and pitch an idea.

AIR and WIR initiatives are one way to amplify the work of local artists, writers, and makers. In turn, if structured with public engagement and programming in mind, AIRs and WIRs can bring unique perspectives and expertise to the Creative Library platform.

Can the community be involved in selecting AIR and WIRs? If we really want to have the community direct how and where library resources should be utilized, why not have the community help decide the slate of AIR/WIRs? Community members could vote online or by paper ballot. If you normally have a jury make decisions like this, make sure that there are some folks represented who are *not* professionally involved in the art world—how about youth and older adults?

EXAMPLE: COMMUNITY-CURATED RESOURCES

Community-led invitations like Library Takeover and initiatives like an artist or writer's residency program are only the tip of the iceberg. Community members can also be involved in determining the library's resources in terms of collections, equipment, and even spaces, if you feel really daring.

Girls Rock! RVA and the Richmond Public Library

FRILL (Free Richmond Instrument Lending Library) is one program we want to share because it's a solid example of a library resource—a "library of things"— that developed due to a close partnership with a community organization. Patty Conway, one of the coordinators of the free music program Girls Rock! RVA, told the Library as Incubator Project about this unique arrangement back in 2017:[11]

> The Free Richmond Instrument Lending Library is the result of a partnership between Girls Rock! RVA and the Richmond Public Library in Richmond, Virginia. Girls Rock! RVA is a free summer camp for Richmond youth, and our mission is to empower girls, gender nonconforming, and trans youth through music, art, and activism. We have hosted programs and events at the Richmond Public Library for four years, with FRILL operating the last two and a half years. For FRILL, Girls Rock! makes our store of musical instruments available to youth ages 8–18 to check out for

free with their Richmond Public Library card. FRILL operates at the RPL Main Branch the first and third Saturday of each month, and on an ongoing basis at the Hull Street branch. We are hoping to expand to additional branches and begin hosting music lessons in the library this year.

The instruments are cataloged in the RPL system, but we have tweaked some of the cataloging to diverge from a typical library item. First, we don't charge late fees. In our nearly three years of operating, we have only had three items go missing, and we decided not to pursue the borrowers beyond a couple of phone calls. One of the things that makes this partnership work so well is that the musical instruments are purchased with donations and grant moneys, not taxpayer dollars—so we are only accountable to our funders, and we all want to increase access to instruments for young people in Richmond, not to charge them fines if they can't bring the items back. We can continuously add instruments to our collection, so if a couple go missing, it isn't a big deal to us. We don't have to be as accountable for our items as a traditional library—because Girls Rock! RVA is not a library! Secondly, items can be checked out for two weeks, with the option to renew for another two weeks—and there are no additional renewals. The item would need to be brought back to the library, checked in, and taken out again if a borrower wanted to extend their time beyond one month. This makes us feel more confident in lending, because borrowers check in with us more frequently than they would with a four-week checkout period.

This resource was developed in direct response to a stated community need:

A few years ago, after the Girls Rock! RVA showcase that we held in the park behind the Richmond Public Library's main branch, several parents approached us and asked how their child could continue to play year-round. Parents expressed concerns that musical instruments are unaffordable, that they worried about buying something that their child might lose interest in after only a month or two, and that their child's public school was reducing music instruction or eliminating it altogether. One of Girls Rock! RVA's founding organizers, Aaron Kemmerer, discussed these concerns with the other organizers. I worked at the Richmond Public Library at the time, so I got to work implementing Aaron's idea to check out the instruments for free through the library. Another of our organizers, Celina Williams, is a librarian at RPL as well, and her input was invaluable as we crafted our borrowing policies and procedures, and always ensured that we prioritized access and used the lending library as community outreach for our camp.

I worked with Patty Parks, the branch manager of RPL-Main, and members of the cataloging and IT departments at RPL's Main Branch to get bar codes and catalog records for each instrument. An artist and graphic designer friend of mine, Annie Warren, designed a logo and letterhead for FRILL for a small fee. Patty Parks at RPL steered me toward a grant for arts organizations in Richmond called CultureWorks, which awarded us $2,000 to purchase additional instruments. Last year, the Harvey Family Memorial Endowment provided us with $7,500 to purchase even more instruments and expand our community presence.

Most of the Girls Rock! organizers and several of our volunteers have staffed the FRILL booth on Saturdays to promote the program. We have PSAs for the program on the local independent radio station, WRIR. We have also had feature articles in the local press to promote the program. The branch managers of RPL's Main Branch and Hull Street branch, Patty Parks and Natalie Draper, respectively, have helped us immensely to get the instruments out into the community. FRILL's main volunteer, Patrick Park, has been keeping track of our library's members and logging checkouts when the library is open, on first and third Saturdays. The circulation staff at RPL has been incredibly helpful and tolerant of our "flexible" approach to checkouts and returns.

Some of the Girls Rock! RVA organizers had the inside track when it came to working with the library, which helped make the process of getting FRILL off the ground more efficient. There are a bunch of interesting things at work here, though. It demonstrates how, when the library embraces a culture of "yes," staff who have creative pursuits outside of their library work feel that they can be a bridge between community partners and the library, even if they don't work in "programming."

The flexibility of the circulation department at the Richmond Public Library and the collaborative approach to developing the resource meant that the end product was something that both the library and the organizers of Girls Rock! RVA were comfortable with. The takeaway from the FRILL example is that, when staff in *every* department feel like they're part of the process, and when you're approaching the work from a culture of yes, the opportunities for expanded, community-driven and community-led initiatives and resources are, at the very least, possible (though they're not endless, because capacity can still be a limiting factor).

Community-Curated Book Displays, Lists, and Collections

Community-led does not have to mean putting in a lot of extra staff time. If your library has an active social media presence, you can ask for book and author suggestions themed around a creative topic, like craft books or books on writing, on a quarterly basis. Make sure the folks that work at the circulation desk know that you're working on this. Circulation department staff tend to have a lot of interactions with patrons about their reading habits and what people are enjoying or not enjoying. They may have a sense of who reads what kinds of books on a regular basis, and they can encourage users to share their current favorites or recommendations.

Once you have a critical mass of titles (which will vary depending on the size of your library), you should "publish" the book list on print, online, or both. You can also make a book display if enough titles are available. You should coordinate with staff who do the selecting and ordering of materials—are there books that people recommended that are not in the library or the library system, and if appropriate, could you purchase some of them?

Projects like this are extra work, of course, but it's work that can (sometimes) get done when you're at the reference desk. You may need to reverse-pilot a similar task in order to focus on the community-curated book list. Is there an e-mail newsletter you're responsible for that just isn't getting the views it once did? Is your library's Twitter account no longer really engaging the audience you want to be connected with? It's okay to let go of something in order to pilot something new.

Note: Obviously, this book-list initiative works well with virtually any topic or genre, and not necessarily only books with an arts or maker focus. If you create an online collection of these book lists, include a link to it on the Creative Library web page. (See chapter 9, "Packaging and Sharing the Creative Library Program," for more on this.) Patrons who are exploring the creativity resources at your library may appreciate the reading ideas from fellow community members.

There are many independent libraries that function as neighborhood archives or repositories that are built and maintained from the ground up by the community. While the missions and structures of these libraries may differ slightly from your own, being aware of and learning a bit about the work that these folks do may help inspire your own efforts.

One example is the Read/Write Library Chicago. This is from their website:

> A city's culture is shaped by the contributions of everyone who lives there and we have the books, newspapers, magazines, comics, zines, artist books, journals, plans, novels, chapbooks, and cookbooks to prove it. We strive to raise the visibility of these documents so that communities can have access to their histories, learn to value the stories of their own friends, families, and neighbors, and be inspired to create and participate on their own terms, right now.[12]

FINAL THOUGHTS: A COMMUNITY-LED YOUTH EDITION

by Laura Damon-Moore

A quick note here about youth-led invitations or initiatives, since there are many folks who may work with multiple age groups. Helping youth groups allocate resources and plan and deliver events or invitations is great experience for them, and it can be a good exercise for library staff as well, to get a fresh take on what's possible in the library.

I'll weigh in with an example from when I worked in youth services at a small-town library. We were in charge of all programming and much of the collection development for patrons eighteen and under and their families and associated grown-ups. The middle school students that we worked with on our Tween Advisory Group (TAG) *loved* Halloween, and so we did all sorts of seasonal projects and invitations, including a Halloween party "lock-in" where kids stay in the library for a designated period of time after hours. One year, the TAG kids decided to plan a haunted house in the lower level of the library, where the program room was. They plotted out the physical layout with maps, assigned parts and roles among each other, and gave me an extensive supply list ahead of time. They organized costumes and makeup, found music and sound effects, and set up a sound system.

Of course there were last-minute issues and various snafus that happened in the lead-up to the event. And there was infighting. Not everyone in the group pulled equal weight, and communication was not great all the time. Ultimately, the haunted house happened, though, and the TAG kids learned a *ton* from this project, and when the next year came around, they already had ideas and edits from their last experience.

Their product was not what we would have planned for them, just like the ideas that came out of Library Takeover were not what we ever would have planned sitting at a computer in the office. And *that's the idea*—that even when the event is not perfectly polished, maybe polish is not really the goal. Maybe some of the invitations *should* be works in progress, providing the space and resources for people of any age to flexibly workshop their ideas.

Notes

1. Public Library Association, "Understanding Power, Identity, and Oppression in the Public Library," 2017, www.ala.org/pla/education/onlinelearning/webinars/ondemand/understanding.

2. American Library Association, "Diversity Counts 2009–2010 Update," http://www.ala.org/aboutala/offices/diversity/diversitycounts/2009–2010update.

3. Tammi M. Owens et al., "'Let's Try It!' Library Outreach in a Culture of Yes," 2018, www.tandfonline.com/doi/full/10.1080/15228959.2017.1411861.

4. Apples and Snakes, "Library Takeover," http://applesandsnakesblog.org/library-takeover.

5. Race and Social Justice Community Roundtable, "Racial Equity Analysis Toolkit," www.seattle.gov/Documents/Departments/RSJI/Roundtable-Toolkit-on-letterhead_1–14–11.pdf.

6. Madison Public Library, "Library Takeover," https://www.madisonpubliclibrary.org/engagement/library-takeover.

7. William Rock, "Art and Inspiration," www.artandinspiration.org.

8. Laura Damon-Moore, "An Artist Residency at Shaler North Hills Library," 2015, Library as Incubator Project, www.libraryasincubatorproject.org/?p=16453.

9. Edmonton Public Library, "Writer in Residence," https://www.epl.ca/writer-in-residence/.

10. Edith Abeyta, "Artist Residency at CLP-Hazelwood" series, 2015, Library as Incubator Project, www.libraryasincubatorproject.org/?tag=clp-hazelwood.

11. Laura Damon-Moore, "Featuring: The Free Richmond Instrument Lending Library (FRILL)," 2017, Library as Incubator Project, www.libraryasincubatorproject.org/?p=19038.

12. Read/Write Library, https://readwritelibrary.org.

THE LENSES:
EVALUATION

TO WEED A TITLE FROM THE COLLECTION, WE USE A NUM-ber of criteria to evaluate whether it's earning its space on the shelf: How many times has it been checked out? Is the information available in newer titles or digital resources? Is there an updated version of the book? Is it in good condition, or do we need a new one? Are patrons still interested in this title? Is it circulating? Do we need more or fewer titles on this topic? (At some point, the 30 titles on instant pot cooking will likely be weeded down to a solid 3 or 5, depending on your library's size, once the fad calms down.)

The point is, books have life spans—and those life spans may be relatively short, especially in most public libraries, where space is at a premium. So we weed. We clear out the old and beat-up books and make room for the new and relevant ones so that our patrons always have access to the best information possible.

WEEDING YOUR INVITATIONS

As we've mentioned throughout this book, we approach invitations (and by extension platforming) with the skills of collection development—which means that *weeding* is a necessary part of creating a Creative Library platform. Viewed through this lens, invitations have life spans just as books do, and building a creative library means viewing your invitation calendar as a dynamic and ever-changing collection of experiences. The calendar should supplement and complement your physical and digital collections, but it can also stand on its own, with offerings that reflect the broad spectrum of interests in your community and different invitation formats to complement different learning styles—from lectures to film viewings to skillshares to hands-on workshops. The platform itself is also an evolving entity, and some pieces of it may need to be phased out, while other pieces merit deliberate growth as patrons use the services and resources you've pulled together, and even work with the library to develop and lead their own initiatives.

Your invitation calendar and your evolving platform will need to be evaluated more often than a physical collection in order to make sure that they're the best they can be. Every activity, workshop, and event on that calendar needs to *earn* the time and resources it takes to put it on. Every piece of the platform needs to be serving the needs of the people who are meant to use it.

This can be challenging, because there's a dearth of standard methods to measure both the hard and soft data necessary to evaluate invitations and suites of services like the ones we advocate for in this book. Weeding physical collections is both an art and a science—but more science. If you pull a weed report from your ILS, it often includes information like:

- The date the title was added to the collection
- The number of lifetime checkouts
- The number of checkouts last year
- The date the title was last checked out
- The status of the book (is it damaged? currently checked out? lost?)

If you pair this information with a visual evaluation of the condition of the book, and supplement it with other info like checking it against core collection lists, you can make a pretty accurate determination as to whether you need the book or not. You might coordinate a display of books that are high-quality but low-circulation to surface parts of the collection that your average patron might miss and thus give some books on the chopping block a second chance, but in general, you *know* what needs to go. This kind of information gives you everything you need to know.

Let's use this lens to look at the evaluation of invitations, specifically. If we apply the same sorts of metrics we use to weed physical collections, we might come up with some data points that look like this:

- The date the invitation series started
- The number of lifetime invitations in the series
- The average number of participants over the whole series

- The number of participants at the last invitation
- The date of the last invitation

These points seem like they could tell us a lot about how many people find a particular program interesting, and whether it's worthwhile to keep it on the calendar. But in practice, that's not always the case. Here are two sample programs to illustrate the issue:

Friday Films	Sewing Skillshare
Four years ago—date started	Six months ago—date started
92—programs in series	12—programs in series
30—average participants	2.75—average participants
5—participants last time	5—participants last time
Last week—last instance	Last week—last instance

If you had to weed one program, which one would you weed?

If you're only looking at participation numbers, you would weed the Sewing Skillshare—both it and the Friday Films had only 5 people last week, but Films regularly pulls in 30 people, and Sewing does not and never will (and chances are, you're not going to get 30 sewing machines).

But anyone who has ever planned a program knows this isn't actually clear.

Friday Films has been going on for a long time, and there's probably a core group of people who always come. But maybe it's on a downturn—as indicated by the five participants that came last time. Do you really want to put in the kind of time to plan thoughtful seasons of films, secure the room and the projector, hold the DVDs, buy refreshments, and come up with discussion questions to lead a conversation afterward? Or maybe there was snow that week, and only a few folks who lived close by braved the cold and the snowdrifts. Or maybe it's a mature program with a dedicated following, and the work you've put in every other week is paying off—there's no way to tell from the "use statistics" metric.

The Sewing Skillshare has the same issue—it's only pulling in 2 or 3 participants, which means a lot of staff time is being funneled into setting up and troubleshooting equipment, planning and advertising the program, and moderating the session. But this one started more recently, and those five participants could indicate significant growth. Maybe it needs some time to develop, or it would benefit from a different time slot and would then start posting higher numbers.

At the same time, this kind of program would be a terrible experience for everyone—those sharing their skills and those learning—if it regularly drew in thirty participants, the way Friday Films does. No one would learn anything, only a few people would get to try the sewing machines, and the group would likely run out of materials. (In MFA programs around the country, where workshop pedagogy and hands-on practice are the norm, classes are usually limited to about twelve students, and for good reason.)

BEYOND ATTENDANCE COUNTS

The above example is meant to illustrate something you probably already know: there are many factors that go into evaluating the success of a program that weeding-style data points can't measure—and attendance is a nearly useless barometer for success. Here are a few ways that these numbers fail:

- They can't take into account how much staff time it takes to organize a particular program.
  - Maybe Friday Films is a partnership with a local university's film studies department, and one of the professors chooses the films and moderates, and all you have to do is get the room and the DVD. No one wants the meeting room on Friday evenings, so it's a great way to boost overall programming stats without a lot of fuss. Or maybe not.

- Attendance numbers can't say whether participants learned something new or felt connected to their community, or yield any other experiential measure we might use when we evaluate our own participation in a program or event and what was valuable about it.
  - What if a program—Friday Films or the Sewing Skillshare—responded to an underrepresented group's interests and created a space to connect? What if Friday Films was being held at a library in an area with a new immigrant population, and the films were chosen to welcome those folks and open a broader discussion? What if the Skillshare was part of a partnership with a local museum for an exhibition of Gee's Bend quilts and allowed a local person with quilting chops to share both the skill and the history of that art form in a black community? What if something about either of these programs changes someone's life?

- They can't tell us what kinds of folks came—whether this program served many different user groups at once, or if it was just one group of people—

and whether the audience reflected the people the program was meant to serve.

- What if the Sewing Skillshare always boasted multigenerational participants, with older adults and parents sharing their skills and hobbies with teens and kids? Or what if it was held in the morning and specifically designed for seniors, and that is a target user group for your library?

- They can't tell us what the ideal number of participants is, or how that might affect the quality of the experience.
  - Five people at the Sewing Skillshare probably allows for a lot of one-on-one instruction and co-learning, while thirty people would be a nightmare. Only measuring a program by participation numbers ignores the fact that some formats aren't meant to draw in thirty people—and that so many people would degrade the experience. Similarly, 30 people at a film might be totally fine . . . but the film where only 5 showed up might have had a deeper and livelier discussion afterward. The experience of those five people could have been much richer because a smaller format allowed them to dig into the film and consider it together.

The same concept holds true when you're looking at broader platforms or suites of services that are meant to respond to creative use. The point is, thinking carefully about what's on your programming calendar, and about the elements that make up your platform, is crucial; and evaluating both of these as you go, and across each year, in order to determine what deserves the library's precious time, is a necessary part of the process. We believe that the skills of collection development apply here, but that programming librarians (and other library folks doing programs) need to come up with a quality set of evaluation criteria that works for their communities—and goes beyond butts-in-seats tallies. Because those tallies don't communicate the whole picture.

ASSESSMENT MODELS

In this section, we will share several models and practices created by real-life programming librarians who have grappled with the challenge of evaluating invitations and balancing hard and soft data. Our hope is that these will inform your practice and give you the tools you need to quantify the importance of a robust invitation calendar, and to continually improve your creative library's offerings over time. Feel free to rip and remix these ideas and make something that will work for you!

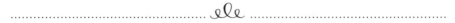

Assessment Tool: Tiny True/False Surveys

An interview with Mallory Arents, Director of Programming, Darien Library, Darien, Connecticut

Library as Incubator Project (LAIP): Tell us why your library found it necessary to explore and implement different assessment techniques for programs besides basic "use statistics" like attendance. What did you do instead?

Mallory: Head counts were not telling us the full picture. We had a sense of our best-attended programs, sure, but which programs were the most *impactful?*

To figure this out, we started with a small, contained series of programs, and we began asking the event attendees to answer a short paper survey. Our Senior Moments programming is a monthly coffee and conversation group developed by the Senior Advisory Board to fulfill an untapped community need of bringing people together and inspiring intellectual curiosity—we started there. Our surveys asked three simple true-or-false questions:

1. I have gained new knowledge as a result of attending this program T/F
2. I have gained a new skill as a result of attending this program T/F
3. I feel better connected to the community as a result of attending this program T/F

LAIP: What did you learn from the surveys?

Mallory: While it was useful to know that 982 people attended a Senior Moments program during this year, it was certainly more impactful to know that 100 percent of the attendees reported gaining new knowledge after attending. That's right, 100 percent. In addition, 66 percent of the attendees reported mastering a new skill, and 82 percent of the participants reported feeling connected to the community during the program period.

While this data would never work in a spreadsheet or normal qualitative reporting system, we used the survey results to construct narratives. By arming our staff and board members with these numbers and personal patron stories, we are better able to advocate for the value of our services and programs. Stories stick with people, much more so than hard numbers.

LAIP: Did your efforts work the way you hoped? If you were speaking with another librarian who was on the cusp of implementing surveys, what would you tell her?

Mallory: Dipping our toes into outcome measurement using simple paper surveys was not a large investment in resources or time. We've used a similar format, three true-or-false questions, to measure other series of programs. While paper surveys worked for our Senior Moments audience, the same questions easily translate to digital surveys. My advice to other librarians is twofold:

1. Think about your audience when designing the questions/container.
2. Hand-sell it. Don't just leave a stack of surveys or send a blanket e-mail; explain why you're collecting the information and how you'll use it.

LAIP: Any other tips for assessing programs beyond use statistics?

Mallory: In addition to gathering outcome data, our team also measures the *types* of events we host at Darien Library. When planning a season of programs, each event is marked in a category (or "glade," as we call them at Darien Library, to go along with our "Dewey lite" nonfiction collection).[1] Author events and book discussions fall under "Literature"; crafts, film screenings, and concerts fall under "Art"; historical lectures and current events fall under "Times," and so on. By categorizing our events before implementation, we're able to make sure that our events are touching on the diverse interests of our community, rather than accidentally hosting things that may only be interesting to us.

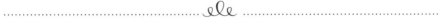

Assessment Tool: Staff Programming Questionnaire
by Janie Hermann, Public Programs Librarian at the Princeton Public Library, Princeton, New Jersey

At the Princeton Public Library, we wanted to be able to tell a more complete and compelling story about what happens in programs to our funders (both private donors and public taxpayers). Being able to have specific examples of how our programs changed lives or even just met a specific need is crucial to the work we do and the story we tell. Public programming serves many needs, and we have to be able to articulate clearly why we are spending time and money to provide programs to the community. In addition, having a more complete picture of our programs allows library staff to easily access data and anecdotes for grant-writing and other reports to governing bodies.

We use a variety of methods to capture information for assessment, including focus groups and surveys (both print and digital) where we solicit community input and feedback either directly after a program or in general. Our most consistent tool is a form[2] that we developed several years ago that is filled in for every single program by the staff member responsible for the program. This form collects information such as program category (book club, film, speaker, author, story time, technology class, etc.), areas of notable impact (civic engagement, early literacy, youth development, cultural literacy, entrepreneurship, job search/career, etc.), and information such as community partners, volunteer hours, whether the location was on-site or off-site, special sources of funding, target audience, audience attended, and much more.

This data is compiled in one giant spreadsheet and we can create custom reports that show, for instance, how many youth development programs we did that were related to technology with a community partner and the attendance was . . . or how many early literacy programs we did that included Latino outreach and at what times, so we can compare attendance across date/time to see if there is a best time to offer such a program. We also have a free field on this form where staff can write anecdotes about the program for future use.

We chose this form because it gives a complete and accurate picture of what we are doing, and it allows us to create unique reports depending on what we need to know for our own internal decision-making or for answering questions posed by government or grants applications. We can use it to make a statement as to why we need more funding, and we can also use it to show how much good we are doing with the funding we already have.

Developing this form and fine-tuning it to be most useful to our staff and goals have taken several years. We are constantly seeking ways to improve it. Our entire team has been trained to be diligent in entering information. It was challenging to get everyone to remember to fill out the form after every single program, but now it is part of the routine, and we do a monthly audit to make sure that nothing is missing.

Assessment Tool: The Reverse Pilot

by Laura Damon-Moore, Community Engagement Librarian at the Madison Public Library, Madison, Wisconsin

The "reverse pilot" is a term I first heard during some scoping meetings my team had with a representative from our city's human resources department. It's basically the idea of a pilot project, where you throw something out there for a set amount of time to see if and how it works, but in reverse. You determine a length of time, say, three months, that you're *not* going to host the program.

Imagine this with a time-consuming, low-payoff program series that you have on your calendar right now (we've all got them). Earlier in my career at a small town library, the program was a Saturday film series that was just not working. Marketing had to be done, volunteers had to come in and get the room completely rearranged, popcorn had to be distributed, and in the end, maybe three or four people would show up, watch the movie, and leave. No added benefit of a community dialogue or discussion at the end, nada.

This was a prime candidate program for a reverse pilot, though I wasn't familiar with the term at that time. So we stopped—or rather, paused—the series for three months, after which we would make a determination about whether to start the series up again, or keep it off the calendar permanently. With the reverse pilot, you put a time frame around it, rather than just saying "this program is over forever." Keep track of comments you're getting from patrons—if no one notices the program is not happening anymore, that probably tells you something.

When you are about halfway through the time frame for the reverse pilot, reassess where you are. Has its absence given the staff more time to work on other projects? Has anyone asked about the program? It may be that you make the decision *not* to bring it back, or else you discover that the patrons who did come really *do* appreciate it, in which case, perhaps you can look at some ways to enhance the offering for another season.

In my experience, there are many programs that remain on the calendar because they're low-pressure, or they're considered a staple, or it feels like they're just one amazing *thing* away from being really great. It is okay to let these go—remember, the invitations the library has on offer are a collection. Use the reverse pilot as a way to gently weed that collection.

Here are a few tips to keep in mind for a reverse pilot:

- *A reverse pilot is* a form of evaluation. It's one last "stat" to look at before a weeding decision.
- Consider what you can learn from this program at the end of its usefulness. What connections have you made during its life span that suggest options for new collaborations and invitations? What did people like about the invitation at its highest point that you can use as a guide or model for designing the next one?

- You may find that the program in a reverse pilot has something worth keeping in your collection, even if the program itself isn't earning its keep. In the Friday Films example, if there are a lot of people who want films, think about incorporating at least one film into other discussion or learning series.
- Prepare front-line staff by explaining your reverse pilot plan and providing talking points, so they can respond positively if a patron asks what happened to the Friday Films and can solicit feedback that you can consider in your reevaluation.
- Remember that invitations have life spans. Your community may go through phases or obsessions just like a teenager. If your neighborhood is super into sewing, you may create a platform around that creative practice, complete with classes and workshops, book lists, and gallery shows of completed work. But after two years, it will be time to evaluate what's still working and what may need to be reverse-piloted.
- Consider shifting ownership of the invitation. If a reverse pilot has shown that a particular program isn't working out, but there are staff or patrons who are adamant that it stay, offer them the opportunity to take it over for one year. This can limit the library's involvement, and sometimes reignite a dying program through the passion of the people who wanted to save it.

Assessment Tool: Rapid Response, Rapid Edit
drawn from Iteration Activity 2, Design Thinking for Libraries

Creating a platform or a new invitation is a lot like prototyping a product. Before you get to large-scale production of your widget, there is a lot of R&D—research and design—that has to happen to make sure that your product is the best it can be. Soliciting feedback on a new process or idea from the people who interact with it (both staff and patrons), and immediately using that feedback to tweak and plan is part of a successful rollout, and the practice is called *iteration*. In iteration, you try something, solicit and evaluate feedback on it, make changes to it, and then try again until your idea is honed into something that really works. Soliciting feedback requires a one-on-one conversation, but you'll want to be able to guide it to the information you need. Here are a few guiding principles to keep in mind when you're in the iteration phase of an invitation or platform:

1. *Define what you're testing*. Is it a particular invitation, or a series of invitations? Is it a suite of resources that's part of your platform? Is it a space? Defining what you're testing will affect who you need to speak with, but it will also limit your scope and keep it manageable.

2. *Choose feedback participants*. Who do you most need to hear from to make sure your invitation works? Staff? Patrons who are older adults? Be clear about why you want each person's feedback. Make a list.

3. *Create a question guide* that will lead to useful feedback. Make sure to order your questions from general impressions, to specific feedback, to a broader conversation. For instance:
    a. Tell me what is exciting about this invitation? Why did you choose to attend?
    b. If you could change one thing about this invitation, what would it be? Why?
    c. What would you like to improve? What didn't work for you?
    d. If you could design your own invitation for the library to host, what would it look like? The sky's the limit.

4. *Keep the following in mind* to make sure you get the best, most usable feedback possible:
    a. *Encourage open dialogue*. Let your feedback participants know that their honest reactions will help you make things better.
    b. *Stay neutral*. You may be really excited about a new invitation that falls flat for others, but you don't want to make them feel bad about their impressions. Remind yourself that their experiences will help you make this invitation just as exciting for everyone else as it is in your head.
    c. *Capture feedback right away*. Have a checklist or form you can fill out easily and with minimal interruption to the flow of conversation, or ask the person you're speaking with if it's okay to record the conversation. The longer you wait to document the feedback you're getting, the more likely you are to lose details that could show the best way forward.

Keep in mind that feedback will show two kinds of changes that can be made—the micro and the macro. Micro changes are those that can be made right away—if, for instance, there weren't enough chairs at the invitation you hosted last night, you can make sure to have plenty of them available at the very next meeting. Macro changes are those you'll want to file away and revisit for planning purposes when you're evaluating the whole series. If you're stuck in a particular room that ends up being terrible for the kind of interaction an invitation demands, you may be able to make some small changes quickly to get by, but chances are you'll have to file that away and book a different room for the next iteration. If a participant points out that a panel discussion lacked opinions from people of color, you can use that observation to check yourself when assembling the next panel or presentation.

.... *ele* ....

Assessment Tool: The Tape Method, or Play/Pause/Rewind/Stop

We learned this tool from Janie Hermann at a Programming Librarians' Interest Group meeting at the ALA Annual Conference several years ago, when she spoke briefly about assessment. It's one that riffs on the reverse pilot method but can be applied more broadly to evaluate a full calendar of programs. We mentioned in chapter 5 that Janie's programming team at the Princeton Public Library is drawn from all departments and staffing levels and regularly participates in programming retreats, where the past year's invitations are evaluated based on performance. Janie and her team discuss each program, how it worked (or didn't), and then they apply the "tape method"—each person at the table gets a chance to press a button on the invitation as if it were an old-school cassette tape.

Here are the button options, in case you have no idea what a cassette player looks like because you aren't nearly as old as we are:

- *PLAY*—invitations that are achieving their outcomes and are anchors in the programming calendar. They're on heavy rotation, everyone is still singing along, and they want them to play again next year.
- *PAUSE*—invitations that need a breather. They may be underperforming, and the pause may be a reverse pilot that leads to a STOP, or they may be more successful as occasional programs rather than continuous ones. For now, they get a pause, to be reevaluated in the next quarter or so.
- *REWIND*—invitations that need an overhaul to continue to be successful. This is essentially a "back to the drawing board" moment, where you rewind the tape and start again. Maybe the idea was worthwhile, but the execution didn't achieve the outcomes you were going for. Maybe a community partner bowed out or wasn't the right fit. It's time to rethink and try something new before hitting PLAY again.

- STOP—invitations that are toast. Because of the deliberate way invitations are pulled together and continuously evaluated, getting to STOP takes some doing, and might mean that the invitation has already lived through a REWIND or a PAUSE, or both. If you get to STOP, it's really time to pull the plug and assess what you learned.

There's one extra element to this method that is an inspiring way to empower the programming team and leverage staff passions: "Everyone gets a Save." It's a practice that Janie uses when an invitation seems to have run its course, but someone on the programming team really believes in it. If they want, they have the opportunity to be in charge of that invitation for the next year—they can save it from the chopping block. It becomes their job to take ownership of that program, to do the work of running it and figuring out what can be done to make it successful, or else it might get cut in the next round.

BALANCING DEPTH OF ENGAGEMENT WITH THE NUMBER OF BODIES IN CHAIRS

So, what do we recommend you consider as you're building your evaluation methods and criteria? First, we would counsel keeping in mind that this is a long-running project, something you'll want to tweak and experiment with over time. It may be important to record different data at different times; consider running your evaluation methods past representatives from other departments, particularly if you're in a large enough library to have a set of folks dedicated to grant-writing and fund-raising. They may need certain kinds of data and stories that you can easily collect in order to make the best case for your library to win dollars. But here are a few pointers to get you started—there are seven, because that's how many horcruxes you have to find and destroy in order to save Hogwarts:

1. **Format**
   What kind of program is this? Is it a lecture or film-viewing? Is it a small group discussion? A one-on-one tutorial? A workshop or skillshare that involves instruction and materials? What number range of participants allows for the best experience? Is this an introductory class (which usually has higher numbers) or an "extension" class for learners who are further along? (Your library should have a "curriculum" that can allow people to continue learning on a topic or to explore widely.)

2. **Outcomes, Mission, Goals**

   Outcomes-based evaluation is a great tool for making sure your invitations meet your goals, whether those are to achieve increased engagement with a particular resource, to build a partnership with another organization, or to fulfill the library's mission in some way. Is this program achieving the outcomes for participants and/or the library that you set out to achieve? And if not, what's standing in the way?

3. **Who Are You Serving?**

   Whom is this program intended to serve? Is the draw multigenerational or targeted to one age group? Is it responding to a particular group's needs? Are you pulling in the people you intended to serve when you planned it? Why or why not? If not, is that a bad thing, or does it suggest an audience and a need that you hadn't considered?

4. **Staff**

   Who is in charge here? Who planned this, ran it, and so on? How much time does it take to set up, run, and tear down? How much planning is involved? Do the staff involved love this invitation and see the benefit of it, or do they dread having to do it?

5. **Cost**

   This includes cash money for materials, refreshments, and so on, but also staff time—how much did this program cost the library in salary or hourly wages? This might seem like overkill, but it could change how you value certain events and invitations. If the big gala costs the library almost as much as it makes, it's time to reevaluate it and consider other options that would have better returns.

6. **Scale**

   How many people came? Are you over or under the ideal audience size for the best experience of this program? What "soft data" or stories can you collect, in addition to numbers of bodies, for small-scale programs that will demonstrate the importance of having these programs?

7. **Insights**

   This is where your boots-on-the-ground people can help by supplying information that isn't data, but is important to know. Which programs are a nightmare to host on the same night? Have people complained about a lack of parking? Is a performer too scary for very little kids?

Thinking globally about the Creative Library platform—the resources, invitations, staff competencies, spaces, partnerships, and services that must come together to respond to a community interest or need—is the next step. Each piece of the platform will be evaluated as you go, but zooming out to look at the platform itself is necessary as well. Here are a few example questions you can apply to this high-level evaluation of the whole:

- What are the intended outcomes for the resources and invitations that make up your platform? Example:
    - Outcome: People connect with creativity resources in the library and in the community.
    - Outcome: People's creative work—either professional or hobby—is enhanced by the library's platform.
    - Outcome: Selected resources (like art books or digital sound-editing software) will see an increase in use after being packaged and surfaced as part of the platform.

- Are you meeting these outcomes?
- How are you evaluating the broader goals of the platform? Is this evaluation effective?
- Are any aspects of the platform underperforming? Is the platform itself underperforming? Is there any feedback from invitation- or resource-specific evaluations that might suggest why?

RESOURCES

The following methods and approaches might offer you some new ideas, or you might be using one of these resources already in your evaluation work.

Design Thinking for Libraries

http://designthinkingforlibraries.com

This is a toolkit designed by the public libraries in Aarhus, Denmark, and Chicago to help guide librarians through the process of creating new services or processes, from information-gathering, to ideation, to feedback and presentation. This toolkit models the scientific method, is easy to use and to customize, and is free to download. The website also has a wonderful Examples page, with videos from projects at the Chicago Public Library and the

Aarhus Library about how the librarians used the Design Thinking process to solve problems or create cultural change.

Programming Librarian

http://programminglibrarian.org

ProgrammingLibrarian.org is a website of the ALA Public Programs Office, and includes program models submitted by programming librarians from around the country, grant opportunities to fund programming, and learning opportunities for professional development. The Public Programs Office also partners with Project Outcome as an evaluation resource for librarians, and hosts webinars and conference programs regularly.

Project Outcome

https://www.projectoutcome.org

"Project Outcome is a free toolkit designed to help public libraries understand and share the impact of essential library services and programs by providing simple surveys and an easy-to-use process for measuring and analyzing outcomes."

Notes

1. For more context on Darien's Glades, check out Barbara Fister, "The Dewey Dilemma," *Library Journal* 134, no. 16 (October 1, 2009): 22–25.
2. A screenshot of the form is included in Appendix B. Janie notes that some information is hidden in drop-down menus.

THE CREATIVE LIBRARY PLATFORM IN PRACTICE

AT THE LIBRARY AS INCUBATOR PROJECT, WE LEARNED A lot from the people who contributed their stories to our website. After reading and writing about hundreds of programs, services, and partnerships at hundreds of different libraries, we began to see a pattern in the ones that were the most sustainable and successful—the ones that came back to share updates about how their experiment had grown and evolved. One teen service model grew to be a systemwide standard at the Carnegie Library of Pittsburgh, and the team that created it documented the process over six years of features on the site.

Here's what we found the most successful creative libraries did:

- **They leveraged what they already had.**
  Libraries that created something new with what they already had were the ones thinking critically about building a platform, not just chasing a fad. Responding to new trends or community interests by repackaging and finding new ways to surface existing content and resources to new audiences is both smart business and a great way for staff to think expansively about the collections and resources they manage. Finding creative uses for, say, expensive newspaper databases that only get a handful of clicks a month, or excellent titles that don't circulate because they are older or buried in the stacks—these might be an important Hail Mary for a quality resource that isn't earning its keep in the budget—yet.

<131>

- **They leveraged the power of community.**

  Libraries that approached the library platform broadly—considering the "collection" of resources, people, and information that existed outside the library's walls, but which could be brought inside—were more successful. When libraries involved partners as active team members in the project of building a platform, the resulting program or service not only created opportunities for people to connect with the expertise of a community group, but also allowed them to bond with other people over a shared interest. We saw this as an extension of the basic transaction of library service, which is connecting people with information. Sometimes the information a person needs is in another person, so creating community—between partners and libraries, partners and people, and people and people—was a fundamental part of the goal, and part of the platform itself.

- **They had a growth mindset.**

  This may be the most important factor, because we found it in just about every submission we received. Whether libraries were using what they had or leveraging their community or both, they always approached the project with a growth mindset, continually evaluating challenges as valuable feedback that could be used to rework or improve future iterations of invitations, the packaging of content, and their relationships with partners and community members. Seeing failures as opportunities for growth and not assuming that past service models were law, but instead questioning how they could be hacked, changed, or scrapped altogether to further the goal of serving the patrons' creative growth was a key factor in success, not least because the folks who worked this way were modeling the creative process in their professional work.

The sections below are a series of creativity platform examples that make use of these guidelines—and surpass them. Some of these are favorites from our years with the Incubator Project; these are libraries that truly embodied "the library-as-incubator idea" and inspired us to think about the practice of creativity as a professional competency in librarianship. Others are newer additions to the Creative Library pantheon who graciously agreed to share some information about their libraries' work. We hope these examples will inspire you to think critically about how to deliver a creative library experience to your community.

LAPL Writes

by Catherine Royalty, Acquisitions Manager, Los Angeles Public Library

The inspiration for the LAPL Writes[1] portal came from working with local authors in our community—we receive frequent inquiries from users looking for guidance on everything from editing their manuscript to marketing their finished book. There is an overwhelming amount of practical information about the publishing process that authors need beyond that initial creative spark. To succeed, they basically need to run their own small business. Our library already had many great resources to help, but they were scattered throughout our physical and digital collections. The LAPL Writes portal was designed to pull all these resources together and thereby make the daunting process of writing, editing, and marketing a book just a little bit easier.

In addition to featuring the traditional recommended book lists, we wanted to make sure our local authors were aware of our other excellent free resources. Our online learning platforms include classes on everything from writing poetry to marketing your e-book. Our events calendar lists author talks and writing group meetings at our various locations where authors can network and get invaluable feedback from their peers. When an author has completed his or her book, the LAPL Writes portal includes access to the Pressbooks software that allows our users to format and design their e-book files and upload them to the library's SELF-e collection.

It is only natural that aspiring authors turn to their local library for assistance—libraries and authors have long been excellent partners. While we may not have the resources to proofread, fact-check, and give individual feedback on every self-published book that comes our way, we do strive to support our local author community as best we can. Curating a dedicated portal for authors, one that features all of our diverse resources, creates a valuable tool both for our users and for staff assisting them.

Why we love this platform:

- LAPL Writes is a truly community-driven platform, a suite of resources, services, and invitations that librarians pulled together because they listened to their patrons and responded to many requests for help from aspiring authors.

- We also love that the platform leverages many resources that the library already had—the research section features databases and lists of books and materials that already existed in the LAPL collection, but curating them to respond to writers' needs made them accessible and usable for that group.
- The other aspect we really love is that there is a curriculum of sorts at work here—LAPL Writes allows for flexible, self-directed learning for writers at all stages of their journey, from research, to writing and revision, to publication and marketing. There is room for people starting out, and people who are farther down the road, to learn and continue to build on that learning

The Labs at Carnegie Library of Pittsburgh

by Dan Hensley, Adult Programming Coordinator, Carnegie Library of Pittsburgh

The Labs is the Carnegie Library of Pittsburgh's (CLP) teen learning labs.[2] Since starting in 2011 with local funding and support from the Institute of Museum and Library Services and the YOUmedia network, The Labs has introduced creative learning to CLP by utilizing artist-mentors to design inclusive learning pathways that can be offered to library users by staff throughout the system.

The Labs has given CLP our Creative Learning platform; this features a set of practices that professional library staff are encouraged to use to engage learners of all ages, plus the equipment, documentation, and professional development needed to support those users in their creative projects. This flexible approach—which emphasizes staff knowledge and ready access to a central collection of equipment rather than concentrated services in a designated studio or maker-space—is a response to the neighborhood-centric layout of our library system. A significant portion of our population accesses the library on foot, and given the importance of equity to our library, we have sought to make Creative Learning available in every neighborhood; even, or perhaps especially, in the more isolated parts of town.

As The Labs has evolved into the Creative Learning platform, one effect has been that these creative services and programs are no longer clearly identified as a branded Labs program. Instead, Creative Learning is incorporated into our general practice. For example, content and equipment that were initially put together as a Labs textile arts workshop might be adapted to enrich a story time, as a cosplay program in Teenspace, or used as an outreach program at a senior center. To the staff, the platform means consistent principles, training, and materials in order to make planning programs easier; to customers, it means a full spectrum of learning to carry them from early childhood to old age.

Why we love this platform:

- We love The Labs because we watched them grow up! We first featured The Labs on the Library as Incubator Project website in 2011, when the CLP's Teen Services Department had just secured a grant to buy equipment and begin running stop-motion animation workshops at a handful of underserved neighborhood branches in Pittsburgh. Since those early days, the level of thought and intentionality that The Labs team has brought to the practice of building and continuously improving their platform has made it a fundamental resource for the entire library system, not just one department.

- The focus on staff training and involvement that evolved in The Labs means that interested library workers at many different branches have the opportunity to learn Labs equipment and share their talents with the Labs audience. This means that these folks are not only engaged with a core service and able to leverage it to solve problems, but also that their personal passions have an outlet at work—something that can build community through personal connections and foster commitment.

- We also love that this platform is using what they already have. The traveling kits of equipment and materials assembled over many years of Labs mean that nothing is wasted and sets of resources can be repurposed for invitations in different neighborhoods, for different age groups, and with different outcomes than what those kits were originally assembled for.

Jax Makerspace, Jacksonville Public Library

by Sara Radovic, Jax Makerspace Coordinator, Jacksonville Public Library, Jacksonville, Florida

The Jacksonville Public Library's Jax Makerspace (JMS)[3] is a place for hands-on opportunities to explore, collaborate, and create. The JMS is a multipurpose creative space located on the ground floor of the Main Library in downtown Jacksonville, and it also features a gallery with rotating exhibits that highlight the local arts community.

The JMS emphasizes making and creating for customers of all ages, whether through arts and crafts, technology, music, or writing. We found that many departments in our library were incorporating hands-on learning in their programming, which led us to take a single area of the library and turn it into a makerspace. We took time to develop relevant programming to encourage exploration, so people could start a hobby here, try it out for free, and see what suits them.

We began offering programs in August 2016, starting with adult coloring and guitar lessons and evolving to classes such as acrylics painting, 3D design basics, and digital photography. The library staff develop and facilitate programs, and we also engage local partners who teach topics like bike maintenance and home brewing, among others. Equipment is also available for self-directed use, such as sewing machines, a Silhouette Cameo, a green screen, and ukuleles. Whether in programs or with the equipment reservations, we constantly connect customers to the library collection. This includes having related books at programs for checkout, as well as displays and bookmarks that highlight the collection, in order to provide a broader spectrum of resources for our customers.

We leave STEM activities out on the tables to encourage self-directed exploration that gets people comfortable with our space. From there, they can take that interest to another level by learning how to sew, how to play the ukulele, and eventually how to produce something even greater than what they thought was possible. We encourage all departments to host their making activities in the space, further cementing the fact that the makerspace is the classroom of the people, the place for consumers to become creators.

The Jax Makerspace continues to expand in scope and services, with virtual reality and digitization services just added and music production currently in development. In our endeavors, we also assess customer interests and feedback with the intent to use this input to design a full-scale makerspace in response to our community's needs.

Why we love this platform:

- The JAX Makerspace's emphasis on art and making is what originally drew us in, but we loved the fact that they used what they already had in order to customize how they packaged and presented invitations and resources for the community. They saw different departments incorporating hands-on learning into their offerings, and they repurposed a space to serve as a hub for those activities as they became more popular.

- There's a balance here between staff involvement and community partnerships to drive invitation design that is instructive, because it essentially allows the community to self-direct their learning. The staff are able to share their skills, local experts lead workshops based on their own interests, and patrons can engage in passive or active explorations based on their own learning styles and interests. It's a win-win-win situation.

ele

The Studio at Anythink

by Mouahmong Yang, Studio Coordinator, Anythink, Adams County, Colorado

Anythink is the public library system for Adams County, Colorado, just north of Denver.[4] It serves the community with seven branches and a bookmobile. The library rebranded as Anythink in 2009 and established itself as an experience library, where play inspires creativity and lifelong learning.

In 2013, Anythink received a $100,000 planning grant from the Institute of Museum and Library Services and the John D. and Catherine T. MacArthur Foundation to create a digital learning lab inspired by the Chicago Public Library's YouMedia project. The Studio at Anythink supports the natural curiosity of the community by providing opportunities for informal learning. Guided by the philosophy that customers of all ages thrive when they discover and follow their passions, collaborate with others, and become creators, The Studio includes both physical spaces and experiences to facilitate exploration and creation.

The Studio strives to meet customers wherever they are on their personal learning path. This is achieved by forming long-term relationships with customers and creating opportunities based on their needs—from passive interactions where customers are observing, to interactive ones where they are creating and seeking to master a skill. To help meet these needs, The Studio partners with local experts—artists in residence—to share professional guidance in a hands-on setting.

Originally, The Studio was developed to create an informal learning space for teens at Anythink's flagship branch, Anythink Wright Farms, and was centered on twenty-first-century digital literacy. This concept has since expanded to include customers of all ages and to reach people across the district. There are currently two dedicated Studio spaces, at Anythink Wright Farms and Anythink Brighton. In addition to these spaces, Studio resources and tools are packaged as scalable traveling kits that can be used to create informal learning opportunities throughout the district. This system allows for consistent experiences regardless of location or staff, and has streamlined the process for onboarding new staff and retaining staff expertise.

The Studio continues to grow organically. With new programs, partners, and resources, The Studio is emerging as a strong brand under the Anythink umbrella. As it grows, The Studio hopes to become a go-to destination for creative people working in all mediums to create and collaborate.

Why we love this platform:

- The Studio's welcoming, supportive approach to learning allows patrons to see it as being *for them,* no matter where they are in their personal learning goals. In addition, The Studio creates many entry points for learners in different media and at different levels, from observation to mastery. This allows a sort of self-directed "curriculum" to develop as patrons gain a new skill and then hone and perfect it.
- The flexible space + kits model is similar to what we see in The Labs and The Bubbler examples—where a special space is nice, but isn't a necessary part of the platform or is essential to deliver exciting services to patrons. Capturing staff and artist-in-residence expertise and packaging this with the right materials and equipment into a kit means the experience of hands-on learning and exploration can happen anywhere with a little coordination.
- People are just as important as spaces or equipment here—and The Studio utilizes the knowledge and expertise of both staff and local artists as part of the "collection" they make available to patrons.

The Bubbler at Madison Public Library

We've talked about The Bubbler throughout this book, and BOOKLESS, the event that kickstarted The Bubbler, is featured in chapter 5 as one of our examples of leveraging staff passions and community partners to create new and exciting invitations and services.[5] As a platform The Bubbler is something special—it is a suite of invitations, partnerships, staff, and spaces that are specifically designed to inspire creativity and promote connection and collaboration among artists and art-makers of all kinds in Madison, Wisconsin.

The Bubbler is made up of a host of component parts, and we'll mention a few of them here:

- *Invitations,* both one-offs and series, that take place in the Madison Public Library's nine library locations and in off-site venues like neighborhood centers, after-school programs, juvenile detention centers, and schools. These invitations range from workshops facilitated by library staff on digital media production, animation, and game design, to workshops led by local artists—everything from screen-printing to illustration to sewing.

- *A professional development initiative for classroom educators.* Called Making Spaces, this initiative focuses on engaging students in maker activities in schools. Teachers get curriculum support, hands-on creativity activities of their own, funding to purchase supplies, and access to a collection of traveling maker kits that move between schools and the library.

- *Teen Bubbler*, a special online gallery dedicated to showcasing the work of youth artists. Teen Bubbler also hosts physical installations and gallery shows at libraries and other locations around the city.

- *Night Light,* an occasional evening event series that usually coincides with a gallery opening and features hands-on invitations, performances, and interactive experiences.

- *The Bubbler Room,* a flexible public space located in the Central Library. The room's features include lots of whiteboard and bulletin board space, a large TV monitor for video art pieces and presentations, a big cabinet chock-full of free-to-use arts and craft supplies, height-adjustable tables on wheels, a sink, and now (due to community demand) a permanent screen-printing sink.

- *The Bubbler Artist in Residence program.* Residencies are usually one or two months in length, and AIRs usually do a combination of open studio and demonstration hours, plus some hands-on workshops and other invitations. AIRs receive a stipend and funding for supplies. Most of the AIRs are based at The Bubbler Room at the Central Library, although some have done "mini-residencies" at neighborhood libraries.

- *An online portal with lots of information,* including the teaching artist database and information for artists about showing their work at Central Library.

Why we love this platform:

- The Bubbler is a flexible model. With the exception of the AIR program, the gallery spaces, and Night Light, the component parts look really different within The Bubbler platform from year to year. The teaching artists who host invitations come in and out as they are available, and one-off programs wax and wane depending on staff capacity and the platform's priorities. There are a few pillars of the platform that remain constant, and because of the brand's strength, other components can ebb and flow as funding, capacity, and community interest shift.

- It's not wedded to a space. Early on, when The Bubbler was just a concept, we had many conversations with Trent Miller and teen librarian Jesse Vieau on what a library makerspace could and should be. We were consultants on the NEA Our Town grant they had won, but conversations with them also shaped our thinking about a service model that we'd come to understand as a platform. While The Bubbler Room plays a big role in The Bubbler platform, it does not have a lot of fancy equipment in it, or a lot of permanent features that would make it unusable as anything but a makerspace should priorities or space needs shift. At this point, The Bubbler without The Bubbler Room would still be The Bubbler, and it would still be able to meet its outcome goals.

·· ℓℓℓ ··

Idea Exchange

This is an excerpt from "Idea Exchange: Building a Sustainable Program Suite" by Jaime Griffis, Director, Programming and Promotion, Idea Exchange; originally published on the Library as Incubator Project, April 2016.

The Idea Exchange (the rebranded name of the Cambridge Libraries and Galleries in Cambridge, Ontario, Canada) supports and inspires our community in the exploration of reading, arts, innovation, and learning. One of the ways in which we strive to create an environment of curiosity and discovery is through our dynamic programming for children and teens. In order to build a sustainable program suite, we needed to acknowledge that libraries of the future are moving from a focus on infrastructure (i.e., print collections) to a focus on space and community engagement. By redefining how we see collection, space, and customer service, the Idea Exchange has created programs that foster creativity, spark innovation, develop human capital, and support lifelong learning.

Our first attempt at redefining how we see collections and space was the redesign of the Children's Department at our Queen's Square (QS) location. The children's collections were analyzed in terms of circulation, but with a twist. Shelf space became "prime real-estate" where collections that performed (higher circulation) received the most linear feet and collections that performed poorly were reduced significantly. The weeding project reduced the QS children's collection by 35–40 percent. And by pushing the remaining book stacks and high-performing collections to the perimeter of the department, we were able to create a large open programming space right in the department itself. No more sequestering these activities in small, out-of-the-way program rooms! Our success was measured in an increase in collection circulation by 18 percent, and we were able to create large, open spaces for families to stay and play in the department.

Staff were able to take advantage of the new large open space and create programs focused on STEM learning and early literacy through play: Kindergarten Connections and Kindergarten Bootcamp are programs that provide families with the tools necessary to help prepare children for their first day of school, and Explore on the Floor showcases 5–6 interactive centers where parents and other caregivers play, discover, and explore with their children. After-school drop-ins carry on this station matrix, where service desk time becomes programming time. Staff actively come out from behind the desk and engage with kids at the centers, recommend books, and answer questions.

These partnerships are present across all levels of programming but are particularly integral to the success of our teen programs. An example of a popular and successful program with great community connections is the partnership between the Idea Exchange and Queen Street Music. By leveraging community mentors in the music industry, we connect contemporary musicians with teens in our Music Is My Weapon program. In this program, teens create, develop, and showcase their songs while getting an inside look at the business side of the music industry, along with the opportunity to network with others in the local music scene.

Teen engagement involves many sectors: corporate funding (to support the hard costs of outfitting a music hub), professional industry participation (to run programs and mentor youth), and proximity to a secondary school facility (for easy access and integration with educational programs). It's also supported by local nonprofits and small businesses with similar goals: making music accessible to all.

By redefining collections and space and leveraging community partnerships, the Idea Exchange has developed a sustainable and dynamic program suite, creating environments of curiosity and discovery for the younger members of our community.

Why we love this platform:

- The Idea Exchange represents something we love: an organizational rethinking of what it means to be a library, one which recognizes that the fundamental transaction of libraries (connecting people with information) can happen successfully in many different ways, some of which we haven't traditionally made room for in the library space. The Idea Exchange literally made room by rearranging the stacks and opening up space for invitations, both formal and informal.
- This platform also considers the broader community of organizations and businesses as part of the "collection." If connecting people with information is the library's goal, then bringing in the expertise of folks in the community to support invitations is a logical method of programming as collection development.

Though this section focuses on how the broader rebranding of the Idea Exchange manifested in children's and teen services, their work extends to all service areas, with a focus on surfacing the library's collections in the community through arts festivals like the Cambridge International Festival, workshops like the Big Weave, and other social and civic opportunities to promote engagement and connection. Check out all three features that the Idea Exchange shared with the Library as Incubator Project online.[6]

Notes

1. Los Angeles Public Library, "LAPL Writes," https://www.lapl.org/collections-resources/lapl-writes.
2. The Labs @ CLP (Carnegie Library of Pittsburgh), https://www.carnegielibrary.org/kids-teens/the-labs-clp/.
3. Jax Makerspace at Jacksonville Public Library, https://www.jaxpubliclibrary.org/jax-makerspace.
4. Anythink Studio at Anythink, https://www.anythinklibraries.org/studio.
5. The Bubbler at Madison Public Library, http://madisonbubbler.org.
6. "Idea Exchange" series, Library as Incubator Project, www.libraryasincubatorproject.org/?tag=idea-exchange.

9

PACKAGING AND SHARING THE CREATIVE LIBRARY PLATFORM

THE IDEA OF PACKAGING MULTIPLE "ELEMENTS" TO develop a library-wide creativity platform is intended first and foremost to invite exploration, hands-on learning, and engagement with the community by pulling together resources and invitations and expanding partnerships and connections with individuals and organizations. There are certainly many internal benefits that come from viewing these elements across the library and pulling them together. Staff from different departments collaborate and have a better sense of what their colleagues are working on; collections and other resources are getting exposure alongside events and invitations; and the library gets real-time, straightforward input and feedback from the community about how resources are being allocated and what should change to better meet their needs.

As you're looking broadly at the possibilities for the Creative Library platform, and what it could or should look like for your organization and within the wider community, it's a good idea to think through some overall goals for the platform. This can also assist you when it comes to marketing and evaluating the platform down the road. These goals don't need to be hard-and-fast ones from the start; as you work with community partners and individuals on how they want to utilize resources and interact with the platform, the goals may shift. That's okay. But, broadly speaking, what do you want to accomplish or reach for? Here are some example goals to get you thinking in this direction:

- The community directs new invitations and resources.
- Circulation numbers of print materials increase by 3 percent.

<143>

- The community engages with the library in order to collaborate and be inspired.
- The community views the library as a space where their ideas are heard and put into practice.
- The community has free, open access to artists and performers.
- The library staff have a deep knowledge of library and community resources related to creativity, and feel confident in making referrals.

These goals don't need to be brand-new or even super-specific to creativity. If you have strategic goals or outcomes that you're emphasizing, feel free to apply these to the broader platform.

A QUICK REVIEW

In the previous chapters, we've done a deep dive on each element that, when packaged together, make up the Creative Library platform. Remember, for your library, each element may not be a discrete thing—the idea is that you're looking broadly at the *whole library* and leveraging connections with the *whole community* to create a robust and sustainable creativity platform. Let's take a moment to recap.

Resources

This is the *stuff*—the print books, the digital library collection, the databases, the audiovisual materials, the tool library, the musical instrument library. It's also the equipment that people can use in the library—the computers, the iPads, the 3D printers, green screens, video cameras, and even the digitization equipment that is used to transfer artwork from slides to digital formats.

Realistically, we don't have an exhaustive list of the myriad ways that creatives and makers could use all of this stuff, but it can be helpful to highlight different resources in order to make users' discovery of them easier. Creative people will always invent new uses for something, so long as they know it's *there*. You can have guides to the Library of Congress or Dewey Decimal Systems handy as bookmarks, or include a link to a guide on the web page dedicated to the Creative Library platform. You can include an "Equipment" section on that page which mentions the obvious creative equipment tie-ins, but some not-so-obvious ones too—the flatbed scanners, the color copier, the digitization equipment. And you can touch on equipment resources when you're giving tours or presentations.

You can talk about your study rooms and embrace the library's role as a "third place," a place outside of home and work highlighted in Ray Oldenburg's book *The Great Good Place* (1989). The library really is one of the last public places where one doesn't need to purchase anything in order to *be* there. For artists and makers of all backgrounds and experiences, having a place to be "apart together" can make the difference between a productive day and a wasted one.

Wherever and whenever possible, you should ask artists, makers, and neighbors what would make their *community*, their *neighborhood*, be a welcoming and engaging place for them to explore and embrace a creative practice. There are places where the library can fill a role, provide a venue, or help make a connection that moves the needle on the community's wishes. Expanding the question beyond "what can the library do" gets people thinking outside of the "book box" and can help inform broader community priorities and work.

Invitations

The chances are really good that, just like the resources in the library, there are already a lot of arts and creativity-focused invitations and events on your library's calendar. This makes it pretty easy to start marketing existing invitations as part of the Creative Library platform—this may be as simple as establishing a calendar tag that groups these invitations together under whatever branding you decide to move forward with.

Establishing the goals of the Creative Library platform will help when it comes to planning new invitations, and weeding the invitations that are currently in play. Don't hesitate to think of invitations and events as just another aspect of the library's collection. It's okay to weed out and streamline the ones that don't "circulate" well or just don't fit the criteria for the evolving platform.

Staff

The staff in the library, across departments, are an incredible asset. Everyone, regardless of their job title or professional experience, brings *something* to the table. Involving staff in the planning process for the platform, to get perspectives outside of your own "work box" or departmental silo, makes for a multi-dimensional platform that invites all kinds of learners—the readers, the doers, the viewers, the explorers—to contribute.

From a logistical perspective, having more staff aware of and engaged in the process also means that there's less work involved in onboarding and training staff. That said, communication and information that staff can refer to internally will be important, especially for the front-line staff who field questions from the community. How you communicate this information will look different from library to library—the staff intranet, a staff meeting, quick one-pagers that "live" at each public services desk, or a combination of these.

Some Questions and Ideas on Staffing

A note on staffing for the managers and department coordinators out there: while we're absolutely advocating for people from multiple departments or teams to be involved in marketing the platform, we also totally get that sometimes the team approach can turn in to doing *everything* by committee. For efficiency's sake, we recommend designating a team leader who can coordinate meetings and action items, with (interested) representatives from other departments who can work on tasks and action items related to their own departments or teams.

What might the makeup of the team look like? Depending on the size of your library, it could look something like this:

- Rep from collection management
- Rep from reference/public services
- Rep from adult programming/public services
- Rep from outreach
- Rep from marketing
- Rep from teen or youth services (if you're including all ages/families in your platform)

The team's makeup could also look something like this:

- Rep from circulation
- Rep from adult programming/public services
- Rep from teen or youth services (in a very small library, it's probably more efficient to include all ages/families)

What If We Have More Than One Library Location?

The answer to this question really depends on how you typically structure large-scale programming models. Here are some items to consider:

- Is the goal for all of the library locations to offer the same or similar experiences and resources across the community, or does each location really function as an independent library, with little or no coordination with other locations?

- If the Creative Library is to be a library-wide platform, it'll be important to leave room for a neighborhood's personality to shine through (not every location will necessarily host the same slate of invitations) while still maintaining a library-wide brand for the platform.
- Depending on how your team works, it might be effective to designate a staff member—or a job description—as the liaison to the Creative Library platform coordinating team so that everyone across locations has a chance to engage in the planning process and share ideas, best practices, and so on.
- Locations could define their role in the Creative Library platform by topic or interest; what these topics are might be obvious given what's already happening and working at that location, or it might be a great opportunity to do an in-depth community survey to revisit what's of interest to a location's particular neighborhood.

Who's on the Hook?

Who the team's leader will be is ultimately a question for managers—even if front-line staff think this is a great model to try, administrators will be the ones making the calls with regard to resource allotment. There might be someone who's an obvious choice, who's already doing this kind of programming or resource development. It might be a manager or coordinator who's invested in the concept and able to look broadly at the platform from a higher viewpoint.

Partnerships and Engagement

Who your external partners are will be key in helping to shape and expand the Creative Library platform. Here are some reminders and tips:

- Working with a diverse slate of partners, both individuals and organizations, helps to ensure that the invitations and resources that make up the platform are inclusive and reflect everyone in your community.
- Partnerships and engagement are a two-way street. Make sure anytime you're asking someone for something, that they are getting something tangible back or out of it (and not just "exposure").
- From the get-go, ask folks what would make their time and energy worthwhile, and avoid over-asking the same groups or people every time.

Community-Led Invitations

Think of an emphasis on community-led invitations and resources as a lens to apply to each element of the Creative Library. Here are some things to keep in mind:

- Supporting and amplifying community ideas and initiatives should infuse everything you do as a matter of course.
- Many of the resources and invitations you'll be assembling into the Creative Library platform may already exist, and some may fit the community-driven or community-led model, while others may not (book lists curated by library staff, or a knitting circle hosted by library staff). That's fine. Make use of what you have and what's already working.
- When considering new resources or invitations, take a moment to pause and make sure that whatever you're adding is truly community-driven (a series of screen-printing workshops that people are clamoring for) or community-led (an artist group that wants to head up an art supply swap in the library).
- Consider ways to ensure that community members have an active say in how library resources are getting used and distributed. Can you intentionally turn over resources to community groups or teams of individuals, à la Library Takeover, so that they can expand their reach and their ideas?

Evaluation

We consider evaluation to be another "lens" through which to view each element of the Creative Library platform—resources, programs and invitations, partnerships and engagement work, and staff.

- In chapter 7 on "Evaluation," we focused on evaluation approaches for programs and invitations, since the models for this kind of evaluation are usually less defined than those for evaluating and weeding library materials.
- Whatever model you decide on—pre- and post-invitation surveys, one-on-one conversations, reverse pilots—be sure to implement it early.
- If there are multiple people coordinating different pieces of the platform, make sure that everyone knows what their evaluation responsibilities are and how to implement them so that you're getting as accurate a reading of outcomes as possible.
- Have one-on-one or group conversations when possible, and talk to as many folks as you can—past and current invitation facilitators; local artists

and creatives; and families or individuals attending workshops and other events.

- When you're able to attend a workshop yourself, introduce yourself right at the beginning and ask people to follow up with you afterward; show that you're really interested in hearing their comments and ideas for pathways going forward.

Okay, so it makes sense to evaluate on a micro level each invitation, each collection of music scores or play scripts, and even your "collection" of community partners to make sure they're representative and reflective of the wider community. But what about evaluating the broader platform—do you do that? Can it be done? Yes, we think that from a big-picture standpoint, it's important to consider the goals and outcomes that you define for the Creative Library, and figure out whether those goals are being met and those outcomes are being achieved. The micro-level evaluations should be considered within the wider context of the overall platform, so that you can pull out best practices, what's working really well, and identify areas for expansion or deeper assessment.

WHERE DOES IT LIVE?

Does the Creative Library platform "live" in the programming department? Adult services? Youth services? Collection management? With administration? Is it truly its own department with dedicated staff, or is it a cross-departmental, cross-location working group? As with all things, this will depend on your own particular institution and what's really feasible.

Perhaps you designate two managers, say from collection management and from programming or public services, to oversee the working group, so it ends up being a joint effort rather than running the risk of being siloed in one department or another. Maybe you go all in and hire a Creative Library platform coordinator, who can liaise with each department that is bringing the platform elements to the table. Maybe you approach it from a marketing standpoint, in which there's an online presence that functions as a visual and interactive way for folks to access all the different elements of the platform, but it relies on existing invitations and resources (at least initially).

No matter where the platform ends up "living," there needs to be *someone* (and it could be more than one person) who is responsible for keeping track of partners, overall platform evaluation, and for accountability purposes.

MARKETING AND BRANDING

The elements for the Creative Library platform are all there—now, how to package the platform in a way that is useful and makes sense to people. You're going to be talking about this platform a lot—you're going to need an elevator speech, you're going to need a good grasp of the goals of the platform, and the staff around you should, too.

How do you name the platform? How do you brand it? We are definitely not marketing professionals, so these are really just things to consider. The example library platforms that we include in this book and on the Library as Incubator Project vary in their approach to naming and branding. Some, such as The Bubbler at Madison Public Library, have a very distinct brand and presence. Pieces of the platform intersect with the library's calendar and parts of the library's website, but it's mainly its own thing. Others, such as The Labs at Carnegie Library of Pittsburgh, have their own web page and "look" but are more wrapped into the library's overall brand. Some platforms have a distinct name (4th Floor, COLLIDER), while others function as an extension of the library's name (LAPL Writes, The Labs @ CLP). Perhaps this is an opportunity for the *community* to help decide what to call the creativity platform.

What kind of marketing presence should the platform have? Size, time, capacity—all of these will factor into this. As with anything you're working to promote, there are endless access points:

- Web page, à la LAPL Writes
- Calendar tag
- Printed one-pager to share with partners and individuals
- Printed brochure or bookmark
- Blog
- Social media, although we recommend picking your social media presence carefully. We don't necessarily advocate setting up a whole new social media suite on multiple platforms because of the exponential work and maintenance that's involved. Embrace one platform and use #tags on others.
- One weird on-brand item; The Bubbler at Madison Public Library has its own brand of (removable) painter's tape.

Whatever you do, marketing-wise, it should roll pretty easily into your current marketing approach without reinventing the wheel. You can start with a couple of key pieces, such as a web page with links (we recommend checking out LAPL Writes as an example), or a one-pager or print brochure with upcoming invitations and other information, and then expand or contract your access points as time and capacity allow.

DOCUMENTING THE PLATFORM

In relation to the marketing question, it's important to document the platform in some way, so that both the library and the community have a chance to share stories about what is being learned, how they're utilizing the creative platform, and so forth. Putting in the time to document platform activities early and often makes it easier when you apply for grants and around budget time.

Here are some ideas for documenting the platform:

- Use a web page, group, or #hashtag on social media, especially for image-heavy media like Instagram. Users can tag and follow your platform's activities easily and quickly.
- In addition to a web page or online portal for the platform, include a blog that features community updates, such as the Glasgow School of Art Library's Hatchery, which highlights different artists, collections, exhibitions, and more.[1]
- Work with artists and writers to make a library zine featuring images and writings inspired by the library's creativity platform.
- Publish a quarterly podcast with interviews, read-alouds of creative writing pieces, upcoming invitations and opportunities, and resource spotlights.
- Make sure to get media releases signed when appropriate, so that you can use images, sound bites, and testimonials down the road.

FUNDING

How have we managed to not discuss funding in depth yet? In many cases, you could get the platform going with no changes to the budgets that support the different platform elements (collection/equipment, programming/invitations, staff, engagement/partnerships). The whole point is that the platform is a strategy for unifying "all things creative," and many of them exist in your library already. You won't be adding a ton of new invitations or resources without

1. working closely with the community to curate them; and
2. letting go of something in order to free up time and finances.

That said, some of the things we've highlighted in this book will likely require additional dollars—an initiative like Library Takeover, for example, or an artist residency (particularly if it's a recurring one). So, what are your options for supporting the Creative Library platform, funding-wise?

- *General operating budget.* Even if you're not including the Creative Library platform as a line item in the budget, the general operating budget will end up supporting the platform through staff time and collection, programming, and equipment/technology budgets. Unless you manage to redirect a significant portion of the programming budget toward new Creative Library invitations, you probably won't be able to finance larger-scale initiatives right away (although it's great if you can!). You'll probably need a few years to demonstrate the value of the platform, and depending on the funding landscape you're working in, the platform itself may never have its own dedicated budget.
- *Grants.* These are great for getting things up and running and trying something new, but are not as great for long-term sustainability. Take your time—grant funding should support initiatives that are community-directed and community-led rather than the library making all the decisions. Start by working on a local or regional level to fund a piece of the platform—a twice-yearly artist residency, for example, or a grant to finance multipurpose equipment like iPads that can be used with a variety of age groups for a variety of invitations.
- *Support from Friends, foundations, and fund-raisers.* Your library's fund-raising arm can be a fabulous resource when it comes to financial resources, but it can also be useful in terms of time donations and expertise. If there is a desire in the community for a big-ticket item or initiative, like a tool library or an artist residency, talk with your Friends or foundation and collaborate with them to determine if and how they can support it. Maybe they will be able to cover a portion of the costs—stipends for AIRs, say—while the funds for related invitation supplies come from the general operating budget.

POLICY CONSIDERATIONS

Much of the way that the library is run relies on policies, rules, and guidelines. We don't really want to bog you down with a ton of new documents, tools, and so on because then you run the risk of getting hung up on the use of these when ideally you're trying to be flexible and remove bureaucracy rather than implementing *more* hoops or barriers. That said, there are some items we want to mention here that can help shape the platform and make it work for you, your library, and the community. If you're looking for concrete examples, we recommend asking the folks in the Library ArtsLink Facebook group and check out the Resources section on the Library ArtsLink website as well.[2] Here are some types of guidelines that might be useful:

- *Gallery space practices.* Giving some thought to how artists interact with the library's gallery space is a good idea, whether you end up with a full-blown selection policy or just rules about what kind of nails people can use in the walls.
- *Meeting room guidelines.* Take a look at any guidelines you have in place now, and think about them in terms of hands-on projects. Are you okay with people painting in the space? Using glue? Glitter? Woodworking? Make sure that how you're promoting your space to the artist community and the community at large is in keeping with what's allowed in that space. Another way to think about this: could you make changes to the space (say, pulling up carpet and replacing it with tile or mats) to open up the possibilities for people who want to make stuff?
- *Art reconsideration policy.* If, for whatever reason, someone files a complaint or challenge to artwork that you are exhibiting, you'll want to be prepared. You likely have a material reconsideration policy already in place. This can be a good opportunity to utilize the expertise of your colleagues and your community partners. Talk with collection management staff and the curators or administrators at a nearby art museum to see how complaints like this are handled.
- *Tour script.* Apply a creativity lens to your library's current tour script for when you're conducting tours with arts organizations, individual artists, writing groups, and so on. Bring up different examples of how folks might interact with the space—for rehearsals and as workspace, in addition to the usual meetings. If you have a gallery space or a makerspace in the library, have a couple of sentences ready to go about how to submit artwork or invitation ideas. You don't have to completely rework your script for each group or around each interest area, but a few examples and mentions that tie in to the Creative Library platform are worthwhile.

OTHER PLATFORMS

Oh, so you thought you were done after planning the Creative Library platform? Well, what we hope is that once you have this model in place for creativity invitations and resources, it will be easy enough to develop platforms around other interests and topics. Ideas for additional platforms include:

- Health and wellness
- Civic engagement
- Racial equity and social justice
- Local history
- Business and entrepreneurship
- Technology and digital learning

There will be overlap between platforms; for example, a journaling invitation series that fits the scope of both the Health and Wellness platform and the Creative Library platform. That's okay—invitations can have multiple calendar categories and tell stories from various viewpoints.

If libraries are all about access, then the platforming model just serves as an additional access point for people who may come for one workshop related to one platform element, and be inspired to try out three others, or to come back when they're farther along in their book-writing or business-licensing process.

PLATFORM ACTION PLAN

It can be helpful to experiment with the platform in a visual way. Use a whiteboard, Post-It notes, crayons and construction paper, or whatever works for you. Start with what you have already. Remember, you're looking at four main elements:

1. Resources
2. Invitations
3. Partnerships and Engagement
4. Library Staff

You'll use two lenses to critique those elements, moving forward:

1. Community-Led Invitations
2. Evaluation

Step 1

Write down everything you have in the way of Resources that you want to high-light as part of the Creative Library. Resources include:

- **Print collections** (books, magazines and periodicals, special print collections like chapbooks and zines, historical or archival collections of photographs or ephemera)
- **Digital collections** (research databases, e-books and digital audiobooks, public online digital collections)
- **Space** (for individuals, groups, larger spaces for community events, galleries, existing dedicated makerspace)
- **Equipment** (digital media production tools, scanners, 3D printers, digitization equipment)
- **People**—in and outside of the library (staff expertise and interests, community members with expertise to share with others)

Wow—you probably have a lot of "stuff" on this list, or spread out on the table-top or whiteboard or whatever workspace you're using. Maybe it feels like too much. Don't worry—a refining process is coming!

Step 2

Now, write down everything you have in the way of Invitations that you want to highlight as part of the Creative Library. Remember, these are programs, activities, events, and workshops that are *already on* your library's calendar. Invitations include:

- **Group invitations** (group workshops, collaborative art, writing, or performance projects, critique groups)
- **Independent invitations** (walk-up stations, take-home or bring-back projects)
- **Off-site invitations** (invitations at community centers, museums, community events, pop-up invitations at local businesses, invitations in outdoor spaces)
- **Invitations facilitated for preexisting groups**

In looking over everything here, you might run into a couple of questions—do we include youth invitations in this list? Does a lecture belong in this platform? Maybe you're seeing some really strong themes coming through:

- We host a lot of visual art-related invitations, but almost zero music or theater invitations—or vice versa.
- We host mostly visual art-related invitations, but our most popular invitations are actually the handful of writing invitations on the calendar.
- We have tons of creative, hands-on invitations on the youth services calendar, but very few on the adult calendar.
- We don't do any off-site invitations at the moment.

Any of the above themes can offer opportunities for follow-up in your community survey, with partners, with patrons, and colleagues. Consider this a starting point for refining your collection of invitations—are there things you see right away that you're responsible for that you want to try reverse-piloting? And there may be some obvious themes to explore and expand upon—maybe you already know, based on what's very popular already, that you're going to focus primarily on visual arts, or writing, or performing arts, or a combination thereof.

Step 3

The next step is basically the community survey process that we talked about in depth in chapter 4, and reprinted here.

The Community Survey How-To:

1. *Start by making a list.* It's easy to begin with arts partners the library works with, but don't limit yourself to only these organizations or individuals. Poke around online, look on Facebook, and always ask the question: "Who else should we talk to?" Ask library colleagues in your area who they're working with—and not just colleagues in similar institutions, either; if you work in a public library, make sure you're talking with academic librarians and school librarians as well. Check out meet-up groups that focus on creativity or the arts.

2. *Remember that it's okay to weed out some community groups right away.* As you're working on your list, you might realize that there are just too many organizations to tackle every single group that could fall under the "arts and creativity" umbrella. It's perfectly reasonable to dive in deeper on visual arts, or performing arts, or writers and writing groups. If you start with one creative segment of the community, it'll be easier to replicate a similar approach with another segment later. If your list feels reasonable and includes potential partners from a wide variety of creativity and arts fields, that's great too.

3. *Meet with people on the phone or in person whenever you can.* E-mail is okay, but a conversation on the phone or in person can ultimately take less time, and makes for a more meaningful connection right away.

4. *Take your time, but make time for it.* As we all know, library work waxes and wanes depending on the time of year and staff capacity. There's no rush on completing the community survey. However, we do encourage you to set aside time to focus on the community survey and the subsequent phone or in-person meetings. When thinking about time management in this way, it can be useful for some people to think about this process as similar to the collection development of library materials—setting aside time to read reviews, determine purchases, manage relationships with vendors, and the like. There's no magic number of hours that you "should" spend on this. Can you spare a half-day per week? You have permission not to have a super-populated programming or invitation calendar, and to "reverse-pilot" some things in order to free up time and head-space in order to dive deeper on community engagement.

5. *Listen and learn.* Each meeting will look and feel a little bit different depending on the potential partner's prior relationship to the library. For an initial meeting, keeping the "agenda" very broad is often a good thing because it keeps you from making assumptions about if and how the potential partner may want to interface with the library and the Creative Library platform. You're not the expert here; they are. Instead of diving right in to the details of what the library is planning and then pitching a bunch of collaboration ideas, "zoom out" first and ask for a broader view of what the individual or organization does, where they fit in the grand scheme of arts and creative resources in the community, and what, if any, gaps they see in resources for local artists and makers. If there's something tangible to offer up in the moment, go for it, but treat this as more of a fact-finding and brainstorming session than a pitch.

6. *Offer to follow up.* Ask if they're interested in staying apprised of the progress on this platform. Depending on their time and interest, opportunities for follow-up range from an e-mail list with updates to more in-depth collaboration and involvement in the planning process.

The community survey process will hopefully help you refine the platform even more, as you learn about what already exists in the community for artists and where the opportunities are for expansion and more exploration. If the community survey step causes you to think differently about what you're offering, that's great—that's you applying the community-led or community-directed lens as you go.

Step 4

The next element to explore in depth consists of the assets right in your own building or organization: the library staff. You may just have a sense, based on conversations and previous co-working, of specific people who might be interested in looking strategically at the platform elements or even in being invitation facilitators. Or you may want people to self-select into an initial working group with the understanding that their involvement may shift depending on overall staff capacity. A sort of "internal community survey" can be used to explore the creative landscape within the library itself. Here are some sample questions to ask in the survey:

- Do you have the opportunity to explore and exercise your creativity as part of your day-to-day work?
- What's one thing that would help you feel more creative at work?
- What's one new thing you'd like to learn?
- How can the library support your creative work and projects?

If you want staff to embrace and participate as part of the Creative Library platform, these questions that support the library community need to be asked—and followed up on.

Steps 1–4 will probably take a *while*, like months or longer, especially in the midst of other work that you have going on. You may also decide that you want to rearrange the order a bit (perhaps swapping steps 3 and 4) in order to determine who will be working on the platform initially, so that you can divide up the community survey responsibilities. Make this process work for you!

Step 5

The elements, the pieces of the Creative Library platform, are there. Now it's time to make a distinct plan for how to market, brand, and document the platform. Here are some questions to ask in this step:
- What will the platform's online presence look like? Will you create a literal portal or landing page for people to access different resources? Will there be an active social media presence?

- Will the platform have a distinctive "look" for printed material and digital objects?
- How frequently will printed material be published? Monthly, quarterly? Who will maintain this material?
- What will the platform be called?

Step 6

Hopefully, in the previous steps, you've been consciously applying the community-led/community-driven lens to the platform as it's taking shape. This basically means not conducting all of the steps in the action plan at your computer or by yourself; and working with colleagues and community members (organizations and individuals) to determine what the creativity landscape is already and exploring opportunities for growth and expansion.

So, step 6 is really an ongoing process. As ideas for new invitations or new resources get pitched, make sure that you're constantly asking some of these questions:

- Who asked for this?
- Where did this idea come from? Out of a community conversation? From a blog or website? From a library conference? From multiple one-on-one conversations with library patrons?
- Does this initiative or invitation amplify existing voices and ideas, or does it (even accidentally) erase or ignore work that's already being done in the community?

We're not saying "don't try *anything* new"; rather, we're advocating that *most* of what you add to the Creative Library platform have some community rationale behind it, that it's community-based, community-driven, community-led, or some combination thereof.

Step 7

Similar to step 6, step 7 is also an ongoing process of evaluation, assessment, and reassessment that you'll do just as a matter of course. We hope these questions are constantly going through your mind:

- What are the outcomes we're trying to measure?
- What evaluation tool or method will work best for the people who are participating in this invitation or using this resource?

- Who is using the data we're collecting, and how available and accessible are we making that data?
- Are we consciously editing the platform elements as we get more information about how it's being used, and being transparent about why and how we're making those edits?

CONCLUSION

We sincerely hope that this will be an invigorating, inspiring process for you, the library, and the community. It's an opportunity to take a step back, and have honest conversations with colleagues and community members about what it means to be creative and how to better cultivate a creative environment not just in the library, but across your neighborhood or town. It's an excuse to reach out to some people you have not connected with yet, and to deepen connections with others. Remember, the Creative Library platform is built to be dipped in and out of, played with, and reworked. It's okay to change it up and to let things go when they're not working. Take your time to ask big questions. We can't wait to see where this process takes you!

Notes

1. Glasgow School of Art Library, "The Hatchery," https://gsahatchery.wordpress.com.
2. Library ArtsLink, "Resources," https://www.libraryartslink.org/resources.

THE LIBRARY AS INCUBATOR PROJECT KIT

The Great Poetry Hunt

"The Great Poetry Hunt" has three goals:

1. To generate poems (and illustrate how poems can be inspired by original sources).
2. To introduce participants to several types of poetry with which they may be unfamiliar.
3. To illustrate the usefulness, versatility, and breadth of your local public library.

The activity is essentially a scavenger hunt. Participants will be given a list of items to find--in this case, poems to write. Types of poems are paired with sections of the library's collection--for example, exploring the Fine Art section leads to the creation of an ekphrastic poem. The length of the item list can be tailored to the number of participants, to level of experience with poetry, and in accordance with the library's resources.

Additionally, many of the "items" can be taught as their own sessions, if multiple days/weeks of programming are desired. Where appropriate, "items" includes resources--links, introductory articles, and reading suggestions--for the type of poem associated with that section of the library. However, the activity is written so that it can be done without any formal knowledge of poetry. (If the "item" is being taught as its own session, participants can be told "Go write this type of poem" because they've learned exactly what it is. If the "items" are part of the scavenger hunt, and participants therefore haven't learned the concept, they are written in such a way that they don't use formal vocabulary until *after* the concept has been introduced and processed.)

An interest in poetry is essential, though.

Recommended readings and resources are appropriate for all ages!

AS A SCAVENGER HUNT

Number of Participants: Technically, any number, but 20 or fewer will allow time for sharing and reflection.

Materials:
- Item list
- Notebook and writing utensil for each participant
- Map of the library/run-down of the DD system

Time needed: 1.5–2 hours

Steps:
1. Introduce the activity.
2. Hand each participant a copy of the item list.
3. Set a time limit: 1–1.5 hours should be enough.
4. Set the participants free!
5. When the time is up, bring everyone together. Encourage participants to share what they've written, as well as add a few words about how they approached the subject material, or how the scavenger hunt has changed their perception of the library and what it offers.

Bonus step:
- Display the poems in the sections that inspired them. Include a note that says "Curious about this person/painting/whatever?" with a citation and recommendations. This will be a source of pride to participants in the activity, as well as being a unique way of drawing attention to the library's offerings.
- Unlike the typical scavenger hunt, it isn't a race, so there is no winner. However, you could still have prizes in various, nonjudgmental, categories (Silliest, Craziest, Most Musical, etc.).
- To encourage collaboration, try pairing up participants before sending them on the hunt.

AS INDIVIDUAL SESSIONS

Number of participants: 20 or fewer is ideal to allow discussion and time for sharing and reflection.

Materials (variously):
- Internet access and a projector; or copies of resources/sample poems.
- Notebook and writing utensil for each participant.

Time needed: 1.5 hours

Steps:
Warm-up, if desired.

1. Introduce the section of the library that corresponds with the "item." Discuss what types of books it includes, where it's located in the library, and why that type of book is important.
2. Introduce the poetic concept, using resources, if desired.
3. Read and discuss sample poems. (Time constraints will dictate how many poems can be discussed: at least two is ideal.) Ask a participant to read each poem out loud. Encourage participants to share their thoughts about the poem. First reactions are often valuable ones. If a participant really likes it, ask them to articulate why. If a participant doesn't like it, ask them to articulate why. Try to come to an understanding. Encourage participants to connect each specific poem to the concept at hand: Why might a poet have made this particular choice? Why write in this voice/about this painting/in this form?
4. Following discussion, direct participants to the section that corresponds to the "item." Give them about twenty minutes to locate some inspiration and draft a poem.
5. Bring everyone back together. Encourage participants to share their work, as well as talk about the process of looking through the library's collection.

Bonus step:
- Display the poems in the sections that inspired them. Include a note that says "Curious about this person/painting/whatever?" with a citation and recommendations. This will be a source of pride to participants in the activity, as well as being a unique way of drawing attention to the library's offerings.
- To encourage collaboration, try pairing up participants before sending them on the hunt.

SOME SAMPLE ITEMS

Get to know . . . Biography

- Find the Biography section of your library.
- Find an interesting-looking biography. In this case, judging a book by its cover is just fine.
- Read the dust jacket. Skim a few pages. Skim until you have an idea of who this person is, what he or she did that merited a whole biography, etc.
- Write a short poem in this person's voice, from inside his or her perspective. Become them. The poem's "I" isn't yours––it's theirs. Introduce him or her to the world, describe what a day in his or her life is like, share a dream he or she had, or just let them talk.
- This is called a persona poem.

Resources for teaching persona poetry:

- "Dramatic Monologue," from The Academy of American Poets (they equate this with persona): www.poets.org/viewmedia.php/prmMID/5776

Reading suggestions:

- Julianna Baggott, Lizzie Borden in Love: Poems in Women's Voices
- Jim Hall, "Maybe That's Yo Pwoblem Too"
- Tyehimba Jess, "mistress stella speaks"
- Patricia Smith, Blood Dazzler

Get to know . . . Fine Art

- Find the Fine Art section of your library.
- Find a piece of art that really captivates you. It can be a photograph, a drawing, a painting, a sculpture, a collage, a digital image, an installation, a piece of architecture––any kind of visual art. Don't overthink it. Trust your gut.
- Write a poem that responds to this piece of art in some way. Describe it, or enter it, or ask it questions. Consider what can't be seen, or what the artist was thinking. Write about what makes it interesting or mysterious or confusing. Write about how it makes you feel, or just write about how thick the paint is or how weird the light is. Write about a memory or person or place it reminds you of. Just respond.
- This is called an *ekphrastic* poem.

Resources for teaching ekphrastic poetry:

- "Ekphrasis: Poetry Confronting Art," from The Academy of American Poets: www.poets.org/viewmedia.php/prmMID/5918
- Alfred Corn's "Notes on Ekphrasis," from The Academy of American Poets: www.poets.org/viewmedia.php/prmMID/19939

Reading suggestions:

(If projection equipment is available, showing the painting along with each poem is a terrific way to understand how poets can look at art.)

- Veronica Chang, "Edward Hopper Study: Hotel Room"
- Sharon Dolin, Serious Pink: Ekphrastic Poems
- Matthea Harvey, "Self-Portraits" (based on the paintings of Max Beckmann)
- Lisel Mueller "Paul Delvaux: The Village of the Mermaids"
- William Carlos Williams, "Landscape with the Fall of Icarus"

Online Form

. . . .

DATA COLLECTION FOR PROGRAM ASSESSMENT

Program Statistics 2018

Please enter as soon as possible once a program or event is completed.

* Required

Name of Program *

Your answer

---

*

Date

mm/dd/yyyy

Program Category *

Choose ▼

(continued)

What time was the program scheduled to start? *

Time

____ : ____ AM ▼

Target Audience *

○ Adults

○ Children

○ Teens

Attendance *

Your answer

Age Groups Attended *

☐ Adults

☐ Children

☐ Teens

If applicable, select the primary area of notable impact? *

Please ask if you are unsure of how we define any of these categories.

Choose ▼

Did the program have additional areas of notable impact? (Select all that apply)

Please ask if you are unsure of how we define any of these categories.

☐ Adult Literacy

☐ Early Literacy

☐ Children's Literacy (K-5)

☐ Teen Literacy

☐ Civic Engagement

(continued)

<168>

- [ ] Creative Outlet/Art
- [ ] Community Collaboration
- [ ] Community Outreach
- [ ] Cultural Literacy
- [ ] Digital Literacy
- [ ] Entrepreneurship
- [ ] Educational Support
- [ ] Environmental
- [ ] Financial Literacy
- [ ] Health Literacy
- [ ] Investment
- [ ] Job Search/Career Help
- [ ] Latino Services
- [ ] Legal Assistance
- [ ] Senior Oriented
- [ ] Social Support
- [ ] Social Media
- [ ] STEAM
- [ ] Youth Development
- [ ] Youth Leadership
- [ ] None of the Above

(continued)

<169>

Impact Details (Optional)
Please take time to fill this in whenever possible. It is very helpful.

Your answer

PPL staff person primarily responsible for organizing this program. *

Your answer

List the initials of staff who worked at this event. *

Your answer

List any relevant Community Partners for this event *
Enter NONE if planned only by PPL staff

Your answer

Where did this program take place? *

O On site at PPL

O Off site

O Area school

Please choose all that apply to this program:

☐ Supported by NEH

☐ PEFF

☐ Summer Reading Program

☐ STEAM

☐ Migrations Program

(continued)

<170>

Was this a volunteer run program? *

○ Yes

○ No

If you selected YES on the previous question, how many hours were contributed by volunteers?
Use this calculation: # of volunteers x hours volunteered = # volunteer hours

Your answer

Please enter the intials of the person submitting this form. *

Your answer

SUBMIT
Page 1 of 1

Never submit passwords through Google Forms.

<171>

bibliography

ABCD Institute. "Resources." https://resources.depaul.edu/abcd-institute/resources/Pages/default.aspx.

Abeyta, Edith. "Artist Residency at CLP-Hazelwood" series. 2015. www.library asincubatorproject.org/?tag=clp-hazelwood.

Alber, Rebecca. "6 Scaffolding Strategies to Use with Your Students." Updated 2014. https://www.edutopia.org/blog/scaffolding-lessons-six-strategies-rebecca-alber.

American Library Association, "Diversity Counts 2009–2010 Update," www.ala.org/aboutala/offices/diversity/diversitycounts/2009–2010update.

Anji Play. www.anjiplay.com/home.

Anythink Studio at Anythink, https://www.anythinklibraries.org/studio.

Apples and Snakes. "Library Takeover." http://applesandsnakesblog.org/library-takeover.

Aspen Institute. "People, Place, and Platform." 2014. http://csreports.aspen institute.org/Dialogue-on-Public-Libraries/2014/report/details/0087/Libraries.

Atkinson, Adam, et al. "Kit: Poetry Scavenger Hunt." 2013.www.libraryas incubatorproject.org/?p=9669.

Batykefer, Erinn. "Featuring: Dominique Dunstan & the Whiteboard Project at the State Library of Victoria." 2015. www.libraryasincubatorproject.org/?p=10971.

Book to Art Club. www.booktoartclub.squarespace.com.

Brooklyn Public Library. "Teacher Lab." https://bklynlibrary.teachable.com/p/teacherlab.

The Bubbler at Madison Public Library. http://madisonbubbler.org.

———. "Teaching Artist Database." http://madisonbubbler.org/teaching-artist -database.

Damon-Moore, Laura. "An Artist Residency at Shaler North Hills Library." 2015. www.libraryasincubatorproject.org/?p=16453.

———. "Featuring: The Free Instrument Lending Library (FRILL)." 2017. www.libraryasincubatorproject.org/?p=19038

———. "Interactive Art Trail at Edinburgh Central Library." 2013. www.library asincubatorproject.org/?p=11753.

———. "Mobile Makerspace at Arrowhead Library System." 2014. www.libraryas incubatorproject.org/?p=14326

———. "Music Lab at the Public Library of Cincinnati and Hamilton County." 2017. www.libraryasincubatorproject.org/?p=19462.

Dent, Deanna. "Engage Your Brain on National Puzzle Day." 2018. https:// asunow.asu.edu/20180125-creativity-national-puzzle-day-how-brains-solve.

Design Thinking for Libraries. http://designthinkingforlibraries.com.

Duggan, Rachal. https://www.rachalduggan.com.

Edmonton Public Library. "Writer in Residence." https://www.epl.ca/writer-in -residence.

Glasgow School of Art Library. "The Hatchery." https://gsahatchery.wordpress .com.

Human Library. http.humanlibrary.org.

Jax Makerspace at Jacksonville Public Library, https://www.jaxpubliclibrary.org/ jax-makerspace.

Kellogg-Hubbard Library. "StoryWalk®." http://www.kellogghubbard.org/story-walk.

Kleon, Austin. Newspaper Blackout. Harper Perennial, 2010.

The Labs @ CLP (Carnegie Library of Pittsburgh), https://www.carnegielibrary .org/kids-teens/the-labs-clp/.

Lankes, R. D. "Library as Platform." https://davidlankes.org/new-librarianship/ new-librarianship-master-class-mooc/ilead-usa-and-new-librarianship -course-content/week-3-libraries/library-as-platform.

Le, Vu. "Are You or Your Org Guilty of Trickle-Down Community Engagement?" 2015. http://tsne.org/blog/are-you-or-your-org-guilty-trickle-down-community -engagement.

Library ArtsLink. "Resources." https://www.libraryartslink.org/resources.

Literary Lots. http://literarylots.org.

Madison Public Library. "Library Programming Application." https://www
.madisonpubliclibrary.org/events/library-programming-application.

———. "Library Takeover." https://www.madisonpubliclibrary.org/engagement/
library-takeover.

Mannon, Melissa. "Orphan Photos to Inspire the Arts." 2013. www.libraryas
incubatorproject.org/?p=12099.

Moore, Tim, et al. "Community Engagement: A Key Strategy for Improving
Outcomes for Australian Families." Australian Institute of Family Studies.
2016. https://aifs.gov.au/cfca/publications/community-engagement.

Owens, Tammi M., et al. "'Let's Try It!' Library Outreach in a Culture of Yes."
Public Services Quarterly. 2018. https://www.tandfonline.com/doi/full/10.1080
/15228959.2017.1411861.

Paul, Ellen. "I Draw New London" series. 2012. www.libraryasincubatorproject.org/
?tag=new-london.

Pigza, Jessica. "Handmade Crafternoons at the NYPL." 2012. www.libraryas
incubatorproject.org/?p=2699.

———. *Bibliocraft: The Modern Crafter's Guide to Using Library Resources to
Jumpstart Creative Projects.* New York: STC Craft. 2014.

Programming Librarian. http://programminglibrarian.org.

Public Library Association. "Project Outcome." https://www.projectoutcome
.org.

Project for Public Spaces. "What Is Placemaking?" https://www.pps.org/article/
what-is-placemaking.

Public Library Association. "Understanding Power, Identity, and Oppression
in the Public Library." 2017. www.ala.org/pla/education/onlinelearning/
webinars/ondemand/understanding.

Race and Social Justice Community Roundtable. "Racial Equity Analysis
Toolkit." www.seattle.gov/Documents/Departments/RSJI/Roundtable
-Toolkit-on-letterhead_1-14-11.pdf.

Read/Write Library Chicago. https://readwritelibrary.org.

Robinson, Ken. "Do Schools Kill Creativity?" | TED Talk. 2013. https://www.ted
.com/talks/ken_robinson_says_schools_kill_creativity.

Rock, William. "Art and Inspiration." www.artandinspiration.org.

Rosenberg, Eli. "Manhattan Subway Becomes Emotional Outlet after Election." *New York Times,* November 11, 2016. https://www.nytimes.com/2016/11/11/ nyregion/subway-notes-offer-a-form-of-therapy.html.

University of Wisconsin-Milwaukee Digital Collections. "Look Here!" series. https://uwmdigitalcollections.blogspot.com/search/label/Look%20Here% 21%20project

Waldo, Suzy. "Pop des Fleurs Winter Pop-up Garden with the Carnegie Library of Pittsburgh." 2016. www.libraryasincubatorproject.org/?p=17841.

Weinberger, David. "Library as Platform." *Library Journal* 137, no. 18 (2012): 34–36.

index